God loves both of me

Jennifer Brown

Copyright© Jennifer Brown 2024

All rights reserved. No part of this book may be reproduced in any form by photocopying or any electronic or mechanical means, including information storage or retrieval systems, without permission in writing from both the copyright owner and the publisher of the book. The right of Jennifer Brown to be identified as the author of this work has been asserted by her in accordance with the Copyright, Designs and Patents Act 1988 and any subsequent amendments thereto.
A catalogue record for this book is available from the British Library.

ISBN: 978-1-916801-20-2

1st Edition 2024.
You can purchase copies of this book from any leading bookstore.

Contents

Chapter 1 A Troubling Start 7
Chapter 2 Independence.. 23
Chapter 3 Finding love, leaving God 32
Chapter 4 Finding God, Breaking down... 50
Chapter 5 Transition 62
Chapter 6 A Broken Jigsaw No More... 75
Chapter 7 Return to Normality... 76
Chapter 8 For the Love of Jesus 94

Chapter 1
A Troubling Start

Let me say right at the outset, I had brilliant parents. When anyone talks of a childhood with very unhappy moments in it, there is often a shadow cast over the home, but this is not the case here. The shadow was cast by something beyond anyone's control and something that would not be truly apparent for 50 years.

I was born on VE day two years after the end of the war. We lived in a prefab placed on the ruins of a once grand Victorian terraced house flattened by a land mine. Growing up in a downmarket part of South London was heaven. Everywhere there were bomb sites, great places to scramble over rubble, tunnel through broken drains, play hide and seek, and other games. The street was our park, no traffic in those days, and kicking a ball was one of my earliest memories.

Then came primary school. I had been christened, although Dad had no great interest in religion. Mum was interested but only sporadically went to church. Despite all this, being christened meant I could go to the local church school, and for the first three years of primary school, I loved it. I was an avid learner, a bookworm, and even at five years of age I was discovering the joys of learning. My three years at primary school were bracketed by two very happy years, where I had a lovely teacher that I was in love with. Year two was with the teacher universally regarded as a strict old bat and I was to fall frequently foul of her caustic tongue. However, she could not put me off. I went to school with an enthusiastic skip in my step. By the time I came to leave primary school to go to the juniors, there was nothing to suggest that I was anything but a normal, energetic boy with a highly developed sense of curiosity and a lust for adventure. Being a church school, a Christian assembly was held daily. This was my first real introduction to God, and I quite liked the sound of Him. The same though could not be said of one of His representatives on earth. The vicar of the associated church frightened me to death, an austere man who would regularly interrogate me as to why he had never seen me in church. The truth was that my parents never took me and, even if I were so inclined, as a 6-year-old, to attend on my own, the bloke who ran the place was the best possible reason why I would run the other way.

However, I liked God. I liked hearing the stories of Jesus, and even though I had a voice that would frighten a herd of cows miles away I loved singing the hymns. I loved His miracles; I loved the bit about shouting at the wind to calm down. I tried it myself a couple of times, but the wind took no notice and just poured more rain on me. A seed had been planted though, and even if that seed were only occasionally watered, it would in later years, continue to grow and take root.

As I passed my seventh birthday, everything was so right in my world. The time had come for me to leave Primary and go to the Juniors. I did not know it then, but the happy times were ending.

Even now, writing these words nearly 70 years after the events, my memories of the culture shock that I was walking into, are clear. My very first day was like walking into hell. I was placed at a desk and chair by the wall. Everyone seemed bigger than me, the noise level was deafening, it was rough, it was rowdy, and I felt totally, completely out of place.

Unlike my nice primary school, the junior school was gender segregated, 35 boys, only boys, in the same class. I was not ill-equipped to be a boy for I was as noisy and boisterous as any, if it had been only me in the class the noise would still have been deafening. I hated, and feared violence, but when all efforts at a diplomatic peace had failed, I was quite capable of holding my own in a fight. I may have been small, but I was stocky, square-shaped, and well-balanced. Many an aggressor would wish he had picked on someone else whilst climbing off the floor. In fact, I can't ever recall losing a fight and was never bullied. It was just that I quite simply felt totally out of place, not a 'proper' boy. Being a 'proper' boy was very important in that era. It was the immediate post-war time of austerity; men were men, boys were boys and there was no allowance for any blurring of the edges. Homosexual men were branded 'queer', sneered at, spat at, and sent to prison if caught in the act. There was no such thing as gender variance, it did not exist, full stop. Any suggestion of it could result in a frontal lobotomy being performed on the poor soul expressing the thought of it.

This culture permeated every sense of my being. To win parental approval I had to be a boy amongst boys and even though I may not have felt like a 'proper' boy, in those early days, that was the end of it. I was a boy, nothing else could ever possibly be thought of, even fleetingly. As time went on so my sense of not being 'one of them' only grew and the misery only deepened.

The great irony was that to everyone else, from casual observer to close acquaintance, I was in every way 'one of them.' The lust for adventure continued to grow and I would be found climbing bridges, exploring tunnels, making houses in trees, and always covered in scrapes and bruises. I was good at football and any time a game was being organised, I was always one of the first to be invited. If I didn't feel a 'proper boy' then I would certainly try hard to be one, often being the loudest and rowdiest in class. I earned more than my fair share of disapproval, something that manifested itself in my parents being summoned to the school on many occasions.

The despair and isolation that I felt even invaded my sleeping hours. Many times, I would wake up from a painful, nasty dream. Often different circumstances but always the same theme. I was somewhere, a group occasion, but wrongly dressed, on the fringes, outcast, not part of it. Often it was a birthday party, everyone dressed up as cowboys and Indians, except me, I would be normally dressed and an outcast. Other times it may be a football match but instead of football boots I would only have school shoes and be cast out of the changing rooms.

The dislocation I felt was immense. I was, at once, very much part of 'the gang' but inside ached to be anything but that. Concentration with schoolwork suffered and the constant lectures of disapproval from teachers caused me to dread the place. By the time the last year of junior school beckoned, inside I just felt a constant churning, mental turmoil. I was thought to be a bright child - passing the 11 plus exam was thought to be just a formality and going to grammar school, considered to be inevitable. It wasn't. The turmoil, inability to concentrate, the dread of going to school, and the feelings of dislocation with my peer group, all came together on exam day. I still remember sitting there in an almost catatonic state staring at the papers. I failed my 11-plus, failed my parents, and felt a failure.

I can't remember much about that summer. I must have woken up at some stage during the 11-plus, as I only just failed it. This led to the opportunity of still being able to go to grammar school, provided I convinced the head of one of two schools that I was the star pupil that they were looking for. The star was not even a dull comet, as I attended both interviews with zero enthusiasm, so they looked elsewhere for their next academic protégé.

That chance gone, the next step was to choose which school to send this most unwilling pupil to. This was before the introduction of comprehensive education. You either went to a grammar school to receive an elite education or went to a secondary modern school as a failure. For a few, though, there was an in-between called a central school, a sort of last-chance saloon for someone to have an almost grammar school level of education after failing the 11-plus. I went to one of those and hated it even more.

This school was only interested in those who strove towards academic excellence and offered zero support to those who were clearly having difficulties with just being there. I dearly wanted to sit down and talk about the turmoil in my head, the feelings of not being part of my peer group, my sense of just not belonging. Instead, it was more snarling letters to Mum and Dad about my lack of attention, refusal to concentrate and inability or unwillingness to take part in class activities.

I needed a friend to talk to, but I had no friends who could fulfil that role. I had increasingly isolated myself from other male friends and talking to females, at least before the onset of puberty, would be something that socially would be totally unacceptable at every level. Boys simply did not do that, well, not 'proper' boys anyway.

Near where I lived was a small park. In this park, there was a spot where three trees, their branches extending to the floor, provided a natural shelter with their branches. It was somewhere I could go, let all the painful thoughts in my head circulate, cry, and try to find peace. One day I realised there was someone I could talk to. He was in my imagination, a man with a big white beard that lay stretched out in the clouds looking down on all of us.

I did not pray; I did not know how. The only 'praying' I had been taught was reciting the Lord's Prayer repeatedly. I just talked to God. I would talk for hours. I asked God to help me but even in my childish distress I knew enough to know that God was not some form of ATM where He dispensed solutions to all our problems. I just knew that I had a friend, a friend who would listen and someone whom I felt was holding me in a great big, cuddly hug. God became my lifeline.

I was reaching breaking point, only God and my ramblings to Him kept me from doing something stupid. My dreams of being isolated from my peer group continued but now had taken an even more emotionally disturbing turn. The disturbing dreams of always being the outsider continued but in the last few dreams I was accepted. I was part of a group, not on the fringes, and was dressed the same as everyone else. However, in these dreams, I was dressed as a girl, looked like a girl and had a girl's name, Jennifer. It was always that name. Where it came from, I have no idea for no one in the family, none of my sister's friends, and none of my Mum's acquaintances had that name. If anyone found out, the scorn and derision that would come my way would be unbearable. Yet another dreadful secret to conceal.

It was a Saturday afternoon. I was indulging myself in the only activity in which my school and myself had a cordial relationship. I was playing football for the under-13 team. I had acquitted myself quite well, scoring two goals and for most of the game, ran rings around their full back, whose retaliatory kicks meant that stud marks now covered my legs. They might have hurt but it gave me street cred with my teammates. I was on a high. I knew the game had been watched by a scout for London Schoolboys, and almost certainly a trial would follow which the school would greet as an honour of great prestige. As I packed up the school kit to take home and be washed, my elation was punctured. Thinking of the plaudits to come from when I returned to school, I was almost frozen with horror at the thought of going back there on Monday.

I did not go back to school. For the next few weeks, I spent most of my school time playing truant, riding around on the London Underground to keep me sheltered from the biting cold November weather. It all came to a stop when a school friend turned up at my house to collect the school football kit which should have been returned long ago. Finding me not there he innocently asked my Mum, 'How is David?' only to be told, 'Fine, why? He's at school right now.' Well, he wasn't at school and the next one to knock at the door, was a school inspector bringing my Mum the glad tidings that if I could do the school a favour and turn up sometime, then they would be delighted if I could also turn up with both parents.

I returned home from my travels on the London Underground, and was met with parental fury. The subsequent interview with the head was met with scholastic fury. With fury all around I went back to school. It lasted a week.

This time I knew that to escape meant escaping both parents and school. I waited until Monday. Mum left me money for my school dinners. I would rather starve than eat dinner at school. I packed enough clothes, food and blankets to last me a couple of days. I crept out of the house and spent the day on the London Underground. That night I broke into a nursery near home. I ate a pack of biscuits from the kitchen and slept the night, leaving the next morning to travel the London Underground. That night I made my way to Waterloo station.

My intention was to meet the boat train. Two days a week a train left Waterloo station for the port of Southampton carrying passengers embarking on one of the transatlantic liners. I had learnt all the details of that train whilst on my clandestine travels of the last few weeks. I knew it pulled into the station at around 5 am to board passengers, departing at 8.30 am. All I had to do was get on the train unnoticed, conceal myself until Southampton, and then when the luggage was transferred to the liner, try and transfer myself with it. How I was going to remain concealed for the seven-day voyage and then get off at New York I had not yet figured out but was confident that I could do it.

Getting onto the boat train platform was easy. I just waited until late at night when the station was relatively deserted, and I climbed over the fence.

Crawling underneath a bench I settled down for the night, wrapped in the blankets I had taken from home. The great master plan though was only two hours old when it was rudely interrupted. Coming down the platform was a station attendant. In his hands was a huge brush that he used to sweep the platform, the collection of dislodged dirt, dust and debris being placed in a large, wheeled container that he pushed in front of him. As this cheerfully whistling member of the British Rail industry approached my bench, he was in for a startling surprise. Thrusting his broom energetically under the bench he was greeted with a large howl of pain. Recoiling, he composed himself before tentatively looking underneath. There, curled up against the wall, was a howling juvenile figure pulling bristles out of his nose.

I was placed into the hands of British Transport police who, realising I was on the Metropolitan Police missing list, transported me to Brixton police station. There I was interviewed by a less than friendly sergeant. Finally, my dad appeared, wheeling his bike, a gaunt-faced, tired and bewildered man. The image of him standing there haunts me to this day. I inwardly cried to God for forgiveness.

God may have been all for forgiveness, but the police and Inner London Education Authority (ILEA) were not. A few days later and I was in front of the magistrates at Lambeth Juvenile Court. The police had gone to town. Burglary, trespass, and theft were on their rap sheet and being beyond parental control was added to the list by the ILEA. The court issued an interim sentence that I was to be remanded for observation and further reports. The place of confinement was a children's home in Southwest London. I had often heard the saying that God works in mysterious ways. I thought arranging for me to be thrown in the slammer was a mysterious way to work. I was not to know then, and it would take a few days, but God had answered my prayers.

To emphasise this was serious business, I was transported from the court in a paddy wagon, a black van with barred windows in the rear. Two policemen sat in front, trying their best to ignore the dangerous criminal sitting in the back. Arriving at the home I was handed over to the reception staff without a word being said to me. I was ushered into the building, given a pile of neatly folded clothes, taken to the bathroom, and instructed to get changed into my 'prison' uniform. The staff came over as kind and caring, which was a big and most pleasant surprise to me.

Having changed, it was time to be shown to my dormitory. There were eight empty beds in it. The explanation was that my new roommates were all at school and I would meet them that evening. I was escorted to the dining room and provided with something to eat. One of the staff sat with me and they explained how the home worked. Its main function was as a foster home, with children left there going to their normal school and coming 'home' in the evening. Only two residential blocks were for confinement, one for girls and one for boys. Yet again, I was surprised that the attitude was more friendly than austere.

For those in confinement, and unable to continue going to their normal school, there was a residential school. That afternoon was assessment time, meeting the principal and writing a two-hour test, consisting of maths, English and an intelligence test, consisting of logic puzzles. I must have finished the test in about half an hour and probably recorded a correct score of 100%. This placed the home in a quandary. Most of the school attendees had severe learning difficulties, probably why they had the behavioural problems that led to them being there in the first place. It was clear that the school curriculum was pitched at a level that was totally inappropriate for someone at my learning standard.

That evening, I met my dormitory mates. I got the looks that every new kid on the block gets, and the dorm bully also had to have his way. Well, he was the dorm bully until he backed me into a handy chair that I was able to swing and crack over his head.

I had been there for all of six hours and was already being marched into the principal's office to have the riot act read to me. Whilst I was being led to the principal, the dorm bully was being led to the sick bay. My contrition was real. Compared to every other institution in my life this one had only ever been kind to me, even if it was so far for only six hours. The principal was stern but not severe. I was led back to the dorm where the other seven boys had decided they would really like to be my friend, even the one with a big plaster stuck to his head.

The following day at the school it became obvious that I was a total misfit and to stay there would be damaging both for me and for the other children. Then I had my first full lunchtime and with it came the realisation that God had listened, and God was caring for me. I had the new boy reception of being bullied in the dinner queue. It was all getting a bit hairy, very rough, when a figure appeared, relative to everyone else, a man mountain. I recognised him as a fifth-form pupil at my school. In fact, I had been very helpful to his brother, someone my own age, a child of clear, prodigious intelligence, but handicapped by what today would be called dyslexia. In those days it was called being thick. I had helped this kid with his homework and other schoolwork. I think like me, I recognised him as being different and being punished for it. We had become friends and I had been able to give him much assistance.

Godfrey, the man mountain, spoke. He spoke to everyone. He left everyone in no doubt that he was my friend, I had looked after his 'bruvver' and he was going to look after me. Anyone wanting a fight with me would have a fight with him. It was the first, and last, physical confrontation I was going to have at that home. In 24 hours, I had become friends with my dorm mates and now everyone else felt the need to also be my friend. More was to come.

After lunch, I was due to be taken back to the school but was instead taken to the headmaster's office. He was almost apologetic as he explained his quandary. I was just too advanced for the school to be of any benefit to me, and it would be wrong to have me there amongst other children who were struggling. I was just one of a handful of children in the home on a confinement order and could not be released to attend my normal school. Would I be terribly upset to be put on a programme of self-learning and spend my days in the library, all on my own and surrounded by books to read? I just cried. My tears were of relief, joy and a love for my heavenly Father, whose mysterious ways had led to what was for me a perfect solution.

The next morning, I attended my first lesson of self-education. The programme I was given broadly reflected what would have been my school curriculum. The library attendant entrusted to help me was lovely. I devoured knowledge. I never let anyone down, they had trusted me, and I was to honour that trust. Every day I was there, I worked hard, and the programme frequently had to be adjusted to keep up with my rapacious acquisition of knowledge. As a bonus, I was allowed to attend the school for the first half-hour of the morning, just for the assembly, where to the huge discomfort of everyone else I could sing hymns of praise to God, at the top of my voice.

Every week I was taken off for a two-hour interview with an ILEA child psychologist. This was an outlet to talk freely, and how I had yearned to be able to talk. I explained my dreams, although not the bit about being a girl, that would most certainly have seen me sent to a mental institution. I explained my self-isolation, and how I felt dislocated from my own peer group.

Three times I went back to court. Three times the ILEA shrinks explained to the court how progress had been made in psychological assessment but at my own request I wanted more time. This was something new to the magistrates, the incarcerated wanting to remain incarcerated.

Three times I was sent back to the home. The fourth time it was clear the shuffling backwards and forwards had to end. The magistrates had to decide whether to send me to a far harsher place of incarceration, a remand home or borstal, or find another way. They found another way. It was being sent home, placed on probation for three years and ordered to attend a psychological clinic at to be agreed times, during those three years.

I was glad to be going home but sorry to leave. In that home, I had met care and kindness, an opportunity to take responsibility for myself, and was able to talk freely about the problems I faced in life. It was not all roses in that place, one member of staff met any deviation from his imposed discipline with brutal violence, but he was only one and thankfully I had little to do with him. There were other minor issues, but the people there cared.

I went back to that horrible school, but something was different. I think that some of the teachers were quite miffed that despite being absent for several weeks I was up to speed with the curriculum, in fact with many subjects ahead of it. I think also there was a 'hands-off' policy, partly due to instruction from ILEA psychologists, but partly due to knowledge of something else that was about to happen. The school was to close. It was merging with a large secondary modern school. The combined schools were to be moved into a bright, shiny new multi-story building called a comprehensive school. Nearly everyone else at the school was broken-hearted at the news of the closure, but at least one person was delighted.

There were also other changes. We as a family were moving home, also moving into a shiny brand-new council housing estate a mile away. I was going to have my own bedroom having previously shared with my sister. A new school, a new home, a new area of London to live in, probation was proving tolerable, and my sessions at the psychological clinic going very well. Ironically, the clinic was the one place, I would return to for help, over forty years later. My Friend, the one that lay in the clouds looking down on us, had truly touched me with his love. The clouds were lifting.

During that summer I went exploring. The lust for adventure that had seen me climb everything in sight, had led to me reading about some rock-climbing outcrops near East Grinstead. One Saturday a Greenline bus took me to East Grinstead and after a twenty-minute walk I arrived at the sandstone outcrop. Having no real idea of what to do, I started climbing, got ten feet off the ground, frightened myself to death and scrambled down. Well, scrambling down might be what fond memory tells me it was, but it was more like tumbling down painfully and crashing to the ground. I walked a little bit further on and tried again with the same result. Then, a little further on, were two young men all roped up and climbing like cats all over a buttress.

I looked on with awe, they started talking to me and before I could blink, they were literally showing me the ropes, how to tie knots, fix a waistband, what a karabiner was etc. Before I knew it, I was roped up and on a very tight rope endeavouring to climb this buttress. I fell off twice but with a bit of help arrived on the top the third time. It was a mind-blowing experience. The exhilaration was indescribable. For the next two hours, I tried my hand at everything, often a miserable failure, but neither one seemed to mind. The ease with which these two highly experienced climbers shared time with a scraggy thirteen-year-old novice, made me feel more comfortable in male company than I had ever felt.

Soon it was time to go home. They explained about another place, bigger, near Groombridge, with lots more people there, in fact they would probably be there themselves in two weeks. They could not say for certain; both were Royal Marines and could be called away any time, but both were hoping to be selected for the elite Cliff Assault Group and would take every opportunity they could to find a bit of rock to play on.

Two weeks later I had found this place they had mentioned. They were both there but shyly I turned away from them, they really would not want to be bothered with me. A voice called out, 'Hiya sprog, you found it then,' and insisted I join them.

We toured the base of the outcrop, and they pointed out different routes. I looked on in amazement at all the hard, tough folk hanging from the smallest protrusions. I stopped at the base of one climb, it looked frighteningly steep. 'Hell Wall' said the one I now knew as Mike, 'graded VS,' VS being a grade of difficulty called Very Severe and well beyond my capability. Mike pointed out all the moves and to emphasise the point, the other one, called Ray, nonchalantly proceeded up it, no rope, no nothing and with cat-like ease. A rope came thudding down. 'Well, don't just look at it' said the voice from above. An hour and multiple attempts later I stood on the top. It would be many months before I attempted something that hard again, but I had learned so much; how to pick out the route, to hold myself in balance, to use counter pressure, to hand jam, to bridge and many more techniques.

Summer came and went. I had met my two new friends twice more and got talking with lots of other climbers. Always with most, there was that ease of being with them. I was learning a great truth about climbing, you can accept anyone of any size, shape, demeanour, anything goes. When you are connected by that rope only one thing matters, 'Is the person at the other end of my rope someone I could trust my life to.' I did not know when or if I would see my friends again, as they had to report to a base somewhere in Cornwall, but I had been to Ray's house in East Grinstead and met his mum. She assured me that anytime I was going to the local rocks I could knock on the door and ask when he was going to be back.

The day of dread arrived. The time to go back to school, but this would be the new school and lots of new teachers. I put on my uniform and my shoes, and with a huge knot in my stomach started the thirty-minute walk to school. As to be expected, when 1,600 pupils came together for the first time in a brand-new school, it was chaos.

I learned a lot of new things. Coming from a school that had less than four hundred pupils we never had houses. Now we did, and I was assigned to Green House and the housemaster was Mr Richards, one of the teachers from the other school. We were also streamed, with five levels reflecting ability, and being a third-year pupil I was in class 3A2, A being the top stream and, 2, being the second best in the top stream. Assembly was rarely to be held in the great common hall, it would be held in the house block, a separate building divided into four.

I could tell, despite all the chaos, who the teachers were from my old school, and who were from the other school, a rough, tough secondary modern school of no-hopers. All the teachers from my old school strutted around in academic gowns. The other lot just wore sports jackets, and the occasional suit. To be honest, given the reputation of the other school, I half expected them to be wearing fireproof overalls, Kevlar helmets and teaching from behind riot shields. As I got to know those teachers and met with new classmates, I was to find out that reputations told lies. Some of the so-called no-hopers blossomed under the comprehensive system to be fine scholars, and I was to meet some equally fine teachers.

As the term got underway and the school settled down, I found my reputation had preceded me. There was a cloakroom incident where several coats were vandalised. As I happened to be in the vicinity at the time I was immediately put in the dock. It took two months of inquiry before the real culprit was discovered and confessed, but I suffered two months of my guilt being assumed by many, and even being told by the headmaster what sort of dire penalty I was to expect.

Another incident was with a maths teacher. My regular maths teacher, Mr Walker, was from the other school and he was brilliant. However, when absent he was deputised by one of my old teachers who did his best to throw me out of the class, having decided he did not want such a disruptive presence spoiling his day. Thankfully, Mr Walker intervened, and I flourished under his teaching.

Then something completely out-of-the-blue happened. It started with assembly in all four houses that was chaotic, with the school prefects chosen to organise the job proving to be incapable of herding four hundred pupils into each of the house blocks.

One of the 'new' teachers I really liked was Mr Richards. He was not only my housemaster but also taught my class in commercial subjects. I will say here and now he was the very best teacher I could have ever wanted for. We also shared faith. I had found out in casual, often conversations before assembly, that we both did not see God as the austere figure of divine retribution, often taught in schools at that time. We both saw God as a loving, generous figure who wanted us all to flourish in the world He had made for us and whom showed infinite forgiveness.

Towards the end of the second term, I was summoned to Mr Richard's study. My mind whirled, what have I done wrong now? What litany of sins was going to be read out to me and how many hours of detention could I be looking forward to? With a horrible knot in my stomach, I knocked on the door and with trepidation walked in when summoned.

He seemed quite calm, quite a novel experience for me to be in a teacher's study, while they are remaining calm. He told me he had been in lengthy discussions with the headmaster about my history, but as far as he was concerned that was the past, and all he saw was someone helpful and enthusiastic in class, and when motivated, a hard worker. I waited for the punch line. No one had ever talked to me like that since primary school. 'I will come straight to the point,' he said, 'I want to appoint you to school prefect, and could you get that bloody shambles of an assembly organised?' I felt as though I wanted to sit down and ask for a drink of water. Last year they were sending me to the slammer with the threat of expulsion when I got out. This year they wanted me to help run the place.

It took me a long time to get used to the prefect badge on my lapel and the green stripe on each sleeve of my school blazer, in fact, I don't think that I ever did from the moment my blazer was altered, to the day I left school. Organising the assembly did not take a lot of thought, it just took being a totally authoritarian prefect on a power trip. Identifying someone from Green House, now called Leigh House, was easy. The tie gave the game away. The school tie was a three-striped one, and the colour of the centre stripe indicated which house a victim, sorry, pupil, belonged to. All I had to do was march around the playground, find people with green stripes in their ties and pressgang them into a working party. A lone prefect trying to arrange chairs and stage for 400 pupils was a trip to a shambles. A lone prefect supervising ten pressganged 'volunteers' was a well-organised assembly starting on time.

It was only a short passage of time before pressganging was no longer needed. Pride flowed through the veins of Leigh House members. We were organised and starting on time, knocking the socks off the other three houses. 'Let's make it even better,' became the mantra. Soon I had more willing volunteers than I could cope with.

It got even better when I discovered that one of my volunteers was a star pupil in the fourth year music class. Now we organised assembly to the sound of gospel and rock and roll being played on the piano. It was strictly forbidden for any pupils to play any piano other than in class or when formally invited, but Mr Richards became very adept at turning a blind eye. The headmaster and his gowned entourage would attend an assembly at each house in turn. On nearly every occasion they visited Leigh House, he would congratulate Mr Richards on such a well-organised turnout, which would then prompt the beaming housemaster to reciprocate by complimenting his star prefect. I think he derived a lot of pleasure in winding up my former nemesis after having to work so hard to persuade him to allow me to be appointed.

Sadly, my newfound success in Leigh House did not translate equally across the board. I needed all my faith and God's love to overcome the sense of peer group dislocation, especially as puberty was coming along to disrupt my serenity further. Some teachers realised I was struggling for reasons other than wilful disobedience and worked hard with me and I flourished in their classes. Others did not and my performance was that of a dismal failure. It did not take long for it to dawn on me that the teachers I struggled with were all from my old school. It was the teachers from the secondary modern school that could motivate, support and bring out the best in me.

The irony of it all is if only I had failed my 11-plus properly, and not been borderline, then I would have automatically gone to a secondary modern school and in all probability gotten a far better education. Even today, I do not need much persuasion to voice my belief in the comprehensive school system. I was not sad to leave school, as I could be more in control of my own destiny, but I will acknowledge the debt I owe to a school in a run-down part of London, and some fine teachers that came to it.

Chapter 2
Independence

Climbing had become my passion. I had become a familiar figure on the sandstone outcrops of South-East England and in my last school year, I had been encouraged to join a climbing club that had a well-organised system of car sharing that allowed me to venture further afield. I kept in touch with my two friends, and it seems surprising now that in those days of no internet, no mobile phones, no email and no social media, we still were able to make arrangements to meet. Sometimes it was pure chance.

One bank holiday weekend I took part in a club meet climbing the granite cliffs of north Cornwall. Descending a gulley to reach the base of an imposing sea cliff, I was startled to hear a voice shout out, 'Oi sprog, what are you doing down this part of the world?.' I glanced towards the voice and saw two familiar faces, surrounded by a lot of other unfamiliar faces. I tip-toed across the rock face with a big grin on my face and spent the rest of that weekend climbing with an elite mountaineering section of the Royal Marines. It was quite an education, in more ways than one. Even though I was a couple of years under the age limit for drinking alcohol in a pub they were not going to allow a mere detail like that to get in the way of the usual post-climbing relaxation!

I had left school with only one exam passed. I had achieved a distinction in the Royal Society of Arts examination for commercial studies. No guessing who was my teacher, thank you, Mr Richards. This achievement was insignificant, the O-Level was the certificate to be judged by and I didn't have any of those. Despite this, I had no problems finding a job. By the time I decided to take a break from climbing and start work, I had three offers. I could be a trainee hearing aid technician, a trainee chef or a trainee salesman at a prestigious upscale outfitter in London's West End. I chose the latter and became something of a novelty, speaking with a London accent, while everyone else who worked there spoke either with the clipped enunciation typical of an English public school education or sultry foreign accents. Yet again, though I may have immediately felt like an outcast, I was to be reminded of God's mysterious ways. It was, after all, a big mystery to me why this rather posh place would want to employ me at all.

I was only there a few weeks when the personnel department looked for its next victim amongst its junior staff. A lot of its senior management were ex-military and military things, such as getting wet and cold whilst marching around aimlessly in the dead of night, were considered to be character-forming. Every year they chose a victim to go on a six-week character-forming exercise. I was asked if I would like to go but warned, 'It would be terribly arduous, involve lots of scrambling over rough terrain, lots of night navigation and, be warned, some rock climbing. You can say No.' For the first time in the history of the company, they did not have to shop around to the point of almost ordering someone to go. The personnel manager nearly fell off his chair when I eagerly responded, 'Have I got time to go home and pack?'

My welcome at the base where this rite of passage was to be held, was equally warm. For probably the first time, they did not have to teach someone how to read a map, for years I had been 'reading' maps in the same way as others read books. When, for the first time, they uttered the doom-laden words, 'Now you all need to learn how to rope up,' the instructor had barely finished speaking, when he noticed I already was roped up. They soon found that with the night navigation, they could take the night off, as I could lead us home, and they appointed me as team leader. I also led a lot of the rock climbing. I returned to my employers to find they had been sent a glowing report on my activities. Fortunately, they left out the bit that another part I seemed most experienced in, was being an underage drinker in the local pub.

I was only back at the store for a few weeks when I was again summoned to the personnel department. With the same feelings that I used to have when summoned to the headmaster's study, I went to the fifth floor with trepidation. I knocked on the door and was summoned in.

He was quite jovial, I was wary. He started rambling about the two great ocean liners, the Queen Mary and Queen Elizabeth. I knew the store had shops on board both, a franchise recently taken over from Harrods. I also knew there was a strict rule about staff having to be over 18, probably something to do with UK licensing laws as anyone sailing would have access to all the bars on board, not something that I would have a problem with.

He then started talking about difficulties he found with staffing, most of the staff not wanting to be away from families, for the ten or twelve days, a round-trip voyage took. I was sympathetic but wondered what that had to do with why I had been summoned.

Then he said, 'Is there any chance that you could fill in for us, do a round-trip?'
My mouth opened but no words would come out. Mistaking the silence for a reluctance he resorted to bribery.
'And knowing that you are only on a junior salary we would give you a very generous out-of-pocket expense allowance.'
My mouth opened wider but still no words so he resorted to further bribery, '...and of course, we appreciate that you do not have the dinner jacket and tie that would be required on a couple of occasions, so we would offer a very generous discount.'
By now he could count my fillings and see my tonsils but still no words. There was no end to his bribery, 'Oh, forget the discount, I will just give you a letter to take to the manager of the dress wear department instructing him to give you all you need.'
Finally, the words came out, 'Have I got time to go home and pack?'

There were two shops on board the liners, one in first class and one in cabin class. Clearly, the passengers in steerage class did not need a shop. They were staffed as a crew of three; two salesmen and a manager. I met my shipmates at Waterloo station, and we boarded the boat train. I could not help but smile at the irony. Four years ago, almost to the day, I was being carted off to the slammer for trying to board this train, and now I'm being paid to do it.

We arrived at Southampton, boarded the ship and found our cabin, which was in the first-class part of the ship. I was travelling in style. The thought of being in male company for ten days filled me with dread but I needed not to have worried. The manager spoke with a sultry foreign accent, but he was more sulky than sultry, totally fed up that for the next ten days, he was going to have to be apart from family just to babysit a pair of lesser beings. He would take himself off to his separate room immediately after dinner and we would not see him again until the following morning. The other salesman was quite happy in male company of a particular kind, and I was not his kind. He quickly found his kind among members of the crew, and I also did not see him between dinner and breakfast.

Left on my own I decided to explore the ship on that first night. I found the top deck, went out into the fresh air, and just stared at the sea and stars. I felt so blessed by my Father God. I found a bar, it was in the first-class part, and I felt totally out of place. I wandered along the deck where the first-class shops were, then down a deck to the cabin-class shops. Curiosity then took over. I went back to the top and methodically walked the length of every deck. I reached that part of the ship called, I think, steerage, or third class by any other name. These decks were mostly inhabited by young students or tourists travelling between the continents. At the end of one deck was another bar, the Beachcomber. I went in and found out that 90% of those travelling in third class were not only young students or tourists but also female. I had often thought of heaven, this time I thought that I was in it!

The Beachcomber became my regular watering hole. I had been given a generous expense allowance to spend on the ship and it would be rude of me not to spend it. The attraction the Beachcomber held for me was not just the same that would attract any young, heterosexual male. It was the sense of ease I found in female company. I just loved sitting there, enjoying a drink with a group of women, mostly American, and talking about my home city, the history, how to use the underground, and learning all about the places that they called home.

It was not to be my first trip. I had only been home for a couple of weeks when I was asked to go again. Apparently, the sulky manager felt it right to give a good report of my work ethic and how I seemed to be popular with many of the customers. The salesman I had been with was a bit miffed that the only people he saw in the shop were females popping in to talk to me. I didn't care. I loved it and on my next trip, I was also asked to write about the trip for an organisation associated with the store. This meant I had work to do in the evening, and was given my own cabin, the size of a broom cupboard, but my own.

My self-confidence, once shattered and broken, was being restored. I was feeling stronger and confident in myself. How my pride would work to destroy me. As I grew stronger, so I grew away from the Person who had saved me, protected me and restored me. It was not a dramatic event, just a gradual distancing and forgetting. I was letting go of the hand of Jesus.

I had been with the store for about a year when reluctantly I felt the need to leave. A brilliant employer, where I had been told that I had a great future with them, but that future meant working Saturdays. I had outgrown the Sandstone outcrops of south-eastern England, and to travel further meant being free on Saturdays. I had negotiated with a chain of men's outfitters that if I worked two six-day weeks, Saturdays included, then the third week would be three days, Saturdays excluded.

It worked well for a short while but then I wanted every Saturday free. I found another job, Monday to Friday, but soon that also was insufficient, I wanted to be closer to the big climbing areas of Wales and the lake district. I was now completely in control of my own destiny, or so I thought, I needed no one and working became short interludes between climbing. I moved to Manchester. I was beginning to exhibit the early signs of what a psychotherapist, many years later, would call obsessional convergence. He was to explain it as a condition where someone has the need to focus on a particular project or vocation with such intensity so as to keep other thoughts and processes out of the mind. It becomes so acute that eventually, the person with it loses sight of the consequences of what they are doing.

I had moved to Manchester and, in between jobs, had spent many weeks camping in the Lake District. I had become a regular member of the local Mountain Rescue team and a regular in the climber's bar of the hotel where the rescue team was located. It was approaching Christmas when a postcard dropped through my letterbox. It had few words on it, 'Fort William Christmas/New Year, Point Five if in cond.' I understood the code. Mike and Ray were planning on being in Fort William between Christmas and New Year, point five referred to a hideously hard ice climb on the Northwest face of Ben

Nevis that is only climbable in very cold and snowy conditions. I had been intending to go home for Christmas, but this changed my mind.

I am not going to go into graphic detail, in fact, I can't, for the memories are too painful to recount in detail. The weather was cold, the snow conditions good, but the forecast was warning of gale-force winds with heavy snow from the Northwest later that day.

We approached the start of the gulley leading to Point Five in darkness, intending to climb at first light when the weather would be coldest and the avalanche risk at its lowest. We anticipated also being up on the top and then back in the valley before the winds got up.

However, forecasts for mountain regions can often be inaccurate. In two hours, the weather warmed dramatically, the stiffening wind whipping up the snow, a loud crack from above and then the three of us tumbled through the air as an avalanche swept down the gulley. All of us in quite bad condition, reached the top by another route, intending to follow an abseil route down to a refuge but the wind and snow created whiteout conditions. We were all badly hurt, the best we could do was huddle together, sheltering by the summit cairn. It was two cold nights of unrelenting blizzard to endure before a rescue extraction could be made. It was only two days later, in Raigmore Hospital, Inverness, that I was given the news that I was the only one to survive.

I could not talk to anyone, friends, family, no one. I could not even reach out to God, my pride had long since convinced me that I did not need Him. I went back to my flat in Manchester and curled up wishing it was me that had died. I went back to work, could not talk, could not do a decent job and after a couple of weeks was told to find another job elsewhere. I was curled up on the sofa when there was a knock on the door. I opened it to find the hotel proprietor and Mountain Rescue team leader from the lake district standing there with two other friendly faces. Sid was a man of few words but strong arms. He gripped me on my shoulder and simply said, 'C'mon lad, you're coming home with us.'

I healed. My orange mountain tent, once a familiar sight under the buttress known as East Raven crag, became a familiar sight again. I joined the rescue team on a couple of calls, nothing serious, but I felt at home again amongst people, who knew better to ask but understood the tears that would suddenly run down my face. I would solo my favourite climb on East Raven, a route called Mamba, morning and evening. Every time I wanted to feel the comfort of my hands on rock and ninety feet of nothingness below my feet.

It was April and the weather had been uncommonly cold with a lot of very unseasonable snow being deposited on the high fells. I was feeling ready to go back to Manchester, find a job, pay my rent and rejoin society. It was about 7 pm. The bell rang, the red bell that would ring for the rescue team. Sid took the call. For a man of few words, he hardly said a thing. We all looked, some of us already putting our coats on.
'It's a bad one', he said, 'Scafell.'
He then told me I had no need to go, what we would find could seriously trouble me, but by then, I already had my coat on. It had to be bad. There were at least three teams nearer to Scafell than us and we were a good three hours away, depending on just how far we could bounce the Land Rover over difficult ground.

We got there and the police, coordinating rescue efforts, were glad of another six well-trained, well-experienced pairs of hands and boots. It was an avalanche. The heavy snowfall of the last few days cascaded down the highest mountain Massif in England, sweeping over a very popular tourist track that had many people on it at the time. By the time weak daylight was starting to illuminate the scene the following morning, we were being told that five bodies had been recovered. I was glad I was there to help with the extraction of the many injured. I had a strange sense of getting my own back. I was in a state of almost collapsing with exhaustion, having worked through waist-deep snow all night, when someone, a leader of the team from Eskdale, pulled me to one side. In that grim place of devastation, in weak daylight, with exhaustion and cold affecting everyone, I had what amounted to a job interview.

It was a short-term contract working with an outward-bound organisation offering outdoor activities for kids who had found themselves on the wrong side of the tracks and had ended up in Borstal. I say kids, some of them were as old as I was, but to me, they were kids and kids deserving of the chances that I had been given. I very soon learnt how to recognise the bullies and they were the ones who so often found themselves in the most precarious of situations. Seventy feet up a crag on a ledge less wide than their feet and being told not to lean too hard on the belay as it might come out. They soon found themselves reflecting on their vulnerability. Meanwhile, kids who had lost complete faith in themselves learnt that they could survive hardship in difficult terrain and that their inner self was made of stronger stuff than they realised. I don't know of one young man who went back without finding strength and confidence in themselves. I loved it but the pay was lousy and the contract short.

It was only later that I could look back and realise how much it had helped me heal. For a few months, I was to put myself back to Father God. The outward bound was based on Christian principles, and it was wonderful to be back again. I find it staggering now to think of the way I chose to walk away.

Back in Manchester, I found another job. I also had a new place of residence, a house in a suburb of Oldham, owned by a lovely Welsh man called Brian and shared with three other blokes. The goings on in that house earned it the name of the house of the rising sun. Brian frequently drove home to family in Wales and now my rock climbing became very Welsh-orientated. I was not going to turn down a free lift to the mountains! For the next couple of years, I made a reputation for myself by climbing the traditional hardest climbs in sight. Turn up, get out, look it up and down, find someone to climb with and then climb it. I was now knocking on the door of the top tier of Britain's rock-climbers.

It was about to come to an end. First, that obsessional drive to pursue goals with almost blindness to the danger that I was walking into led me to nearly my greatest folly. I had a climb on my bucket list, a route forced up a crag in the Llanberis Valley by the legendary pair of Joe Brown and Don Whillans. I could find no one to climb with. Friday I was coming back home to Oldham and this damp Thursday morning was my last day.

I walked up to the crag and stared forlornly upwards at the route, marvelling at the skill and daring of the pioneer climbers. I started climbing it, and at 50 feet I realised my folly but could not stop climbing. I was now in a stupid situation. Climbing back down was most definitely not possible. Climbing up was probably suicidal, but hey, I had a chance at survival. I continued upwards, the exposure, the sense of being high with nothing around you, almost paralysing. My tired fingers were losing strength. I thought of the guidebook, I was still a long way from the so-called 'thank God' holds that signify the easing of difficulties and the end of the climb. My mind swam, I had thoughts of just letting go and letting the inevitable happen. With numbing fingers and an even more numbing mind, I called on my last reserves of physical and mental strength for that long reach so well described by the original pioneers, a lunge, a scrabble, then the top.

I sat at the top for what seemed like hours. My heart pounded away; my mind swamped with 'what might have been.' My hands were numb, cut and bleeding as I made my way down. I was shaken to my very core. I walked to the road and started the long trek into Llanberis. The next morning I met Brian and came home. It was my last act of dancing with danger on the crags of Britain.

Chapter 3
Finding love, leaving God

The following day a friend came round. He announced the exciting news that he knew of a party a group of young ladies were having. He then gave us the bad news that we were not invited. I was emotionally drained, and so physically exhausted that I couldn't care less, but not being invited was a red rag to a bull. I would just have to turn up and gate crash.

We duly arrived at the address given, rang the bell and walked straight in as the door was opened. Facing me was a curly-haired young lady whom I understood was the hostess. I thought I would talk to her, apologise for my totally ungentlemanly behaviour of just barging in, and offer her a chilled tonic water as an apology. Ok, forget all that, I thought I would chat her up. At 5 am in the morning, I still sat on the sofa chatting her up. Her name was Jo, and I knew then that she was to be my partner for life.

It was to be a whirlwind marriage, no point saving up for something splendid. My finances were so parlous that the sum value of all my worldly assets was significantly less than the money I had owed from borrowings to finance my climbing. To share joint assets, or rather for me to share Jo's assets and her my debts, seemed to make sense. Before any wedding though I had to run the gauntlet of meeting the parents.

I was to meet two people whom I came to love as much as I loved anyone in my life. I was to find that I was truly blessed by my in-laws, but it was not going to be an easy ride. I first met Jo's Dad, a very devout Catholic. The very first question he put to me, even before saying, 'Hello, I'm Jo's father,' was 'What religion are you?' Somewhat startled I told him I was Christian; it was about all I could think of in that moment. I then had a short lecture on the only true religion being Roman Catholic. Realising now what he meant by religion, I cheerfully mentioned that I was Protestant, before realising that was not the best thing to say to someone who passionately supported the nationalist cause in Northern Ireland.

That hiccup aside, my relationship with them blossomed. The question of religion though did not go away in my head. I was reminded of the deep divides that differing religions can cause in society, and this had a subtle effect of moving me further away from God and closer towards even agnosticism.

I was beyond skint. My attempts at finding jobs were reasonably successful but my attempts at keeping them less so. We were married, in a Catholic Church, and the reception was largely provided by friends and family; Brian provided the music with his accordion, others chipped in to buy food and drink, and someone else provided the transport for me to whisk Jo away on a brief honeymoon in a Manchester hotel.

At the time of our wedding, I had a job. I was working as a retail assistant with a nationwide chain of domestic electrical appliance suppliers. It was they who had provided me with the transport for our wedding. When I returned to work, I found that I no longer had a job, due to them preferring that I ask them first, rather than just 'borrow' the company van!

A few short weeks and about five jobs later, we learned the news that Jo was pregnant, and children were on the way, two of them, twins. We had managed to find a flat on a council estate in a nice brand-new block. It was a cold winter, and we were glad of the modern central heating and insulated windows, having until now endured draughty, leaky bedsits. Then typically the babies arrived a few weeks early. Now I was not only penniless and out of work, again, I had a wife who could no longer work, and also two children to feed. Our circumstances were desperate, but we were happy, especially someone who had spent his entire life persuading himself and everyone else that he was fully male. Being a father only emphasised the point.

A few more months and the finances were critical to the point that the threatening letters from Oldham Borough Council for non-payment of rent had now become eviction notices. Thankfully in the very week that my children and wife were to be taken into care and myself rendered homeless, Jo found a job as a residential warden of a care home. This job came with a two-bedroomed flat. Naturally, my pride made me congratulate myself for seeing the advertised job, nothing to do with Jo winning over her employers or, more importantly, our Father God. I might have moved away from Him but looking back now, with pride taken from my eyes, it is obvious that He never moved from our side. With a lot of help from friends, we managed to empty our flat and move all our worldly belongings into our new flat, just a few hours before the bailiffs were due to arrive.

This flat had a study. I was very aware that my job prospects were bleak because of my equally bleak collection of academic bits of paper. A meaningless certificate and a chequered job history were not very appealing to employers who could pick and choose, the country was now in recession and jobs scarce. Along came the open university. I did not need O-levels or any other level to sign up. I just needed somewhere to study and that had been provided.

I was desperate to study. My mind was short of things to occupy it, to keep it closed to any questioning as to why I felt so different, so alienated from feeling 'a man.' Then my educational fees fell into arrears and the OU was about to cease my studies. In the meantime, through impudence and subterfuge, I had found a job, my unorthodox approach appealing to the boss when he found out.

A few short weeks into this job, as a retail analyst with an oil company, the country was plunged into crisis as supplies of crude oil from the Gulf states almost dried up. It was the time of the Yom Kippur war between Israel and its Arab neighbours, and the West was being punished for assisting Israel. The company needed a mastermind to sit at one of the oil terminals balancing supplies with supply. However, as the location of the nearest terminal in the north of England was part of the nation's key strategic reserves network, the mastermind also had to be approved by state security.

None of the proposed masterminds from the company's head office had that security. I did, part of my crisscrossing the Atlantic a few years earlier involved aspects that required the necessary approvals. I mentioned it to my boss who then fought my case, and the unproved mastermind was seconded to fulfil what everyone recognised as a hugely demanding task.

Apparently, I did rather well. My boss recommended me to the corporate planning department. A financial career was the last thing I had thought of, or wanted, but not for the first time in my life was I to find someone who could judge me better than I could and be firm in directing me down a better path. Grudgingly I agreed, my wounded pride being helped to heal enormously by a pay rise and a very generous gesture of funding my future studies with the OU, which I was able to complete in the following year, just as my career with this company was coming to an end.

The end, for once, had nothing to do with me but everything to do with actions thousands of miles away. The restrictions on oil supplies had plunged many European economies into recession, and the company I worked for had to consolidate and reduce its number of regional offices. Now, confirmed as a trainee mastermind I was not parted with, but the writing was on the wall. A phone call from a recruitment agency invited me to pop along for an interview with a subsidiary of an American multinational. They wanted a financial analyst for their corporate planning department.

Within a few weeks of joining this company, I was asked/told to move to the USA. This I could not do. One of my sons had been born with difficulties, later to be diagnosed as autism, and such a move simply could not be considered. The man in America had a think, a Master's Degree in Business Administration (MBA) was essential for my future progression. I hinted that in Manchester we had an excellent business school and that I could do an external Masters.
'Can you work and study at the same time,' he asked.
I smiled inwardly. I had to; anything less would give me time for my mind to dwell on feelings that I was desperately trying not to go near.

With the new job came a big pay rise, still not enough to entertain paying off debts, but enough to go further into debt! My salary was sufficient to be approved for a mortgage, and all I needed was a deposit to buy a house. I had recently acquired one of those new, modern things recently introduced called a credit card. I basically borrowed against my credit. We were now even more in debt than ever, but I had a well-paid job, and we were at least on the housing ladder.

My well-paid job had a limitation though. With refusing to relocate to the USA I felt as though my promotion prospects were limited. I needed a promotion, both to help pay our huge debt load and to keep me busy, as those thoughts of being different just would not stop nagging me. One night the phone rang. It was the recruitment agency. A large, ailing British multinational called British Leyland was recruiting. They wanted a senior financial analyst in their corporate planning department, and was I interested?

I indicated my interest but heard nothing. Then about three weeks after being contacted by the headhunters an offer of employment arrived through my letterbox. I was a little bemused and checked the envelope, yes, it was addressed to me. I read the offer, I would really have liked an interview or two, so I could ask what I was letting myself in for, but then looked at the salary, the conditions, the offer of a car, and signed my agreement.

I started the next month. This company was a mess. My first indication of how much of a mess came when I turned up at reception, offer letter in hand and no idea who my future boss was. The receptionist looked at the letter, made a phone call, then a few minutes later a beaming face that I had never seen before came bouncing down the stairs, hand outstretched, with a cheery, 'David, good morning, nice to see you again.' We went upstairs to his office.

Formalities over, it was, 'Let me take you to your line manager.' Thanks to my gift for reading upside-down memos, I was able to respond with, 'Thank you, Frank,' avoiding the embarrassment of having to admit I did not know who the hell this guy was. Approaching another office, it was opened by another beaming face that I had never seen before. Again, it was hand outstretched with a 'Great to see you again, David.'

Finally, sitting at my desk, after being introduced to my new colleagues, the buzz of chatter suddenly quietened down. The big chief, the Divisional Financial Director, had entered the building. Eager to introduce himself to one of his new minions he strode over, hand outstretched, 'Good to see you again.' I just inwardly groaned as I held out my hand to the man who introduced himself as Ken. I think Ken had called me Ted but by that time, I was past caring about what sort of shambles I had wandered into and just looked for a task that I could get my teeth into.

The company being in a mess suited me, it just meant that I was kept very busy. I could prove myself over and over again and get the promotions I needed to keep the wolf, or the bailiffs, from the door. My first opportunity came when someone was needed to be parachuted into a subsidiary two hundred miles away. With a fortnight to go before an important accounting deadline, this company was way behind in its planning, and the financial controller had abruptly left. It was supposed to be a hopeless task, but I was asked to 'go and do' my best. The obsessional need to keep busy took over and working enormous hours the task was achieved on time.

Then I was asked to move my job, home, family, and dogs to another part of the country where another subsidiary needed a financial controller. Another mess sorted and this became the pattern for the next ten years, each move being a bigger subsidiary, a bigger job to do and a bigger pay grade to go with it. If my debt mountain at the beginning was of Himalayan Mountain range proportions, at the end of ten years they were only of a single Everest size. The cost though to my family, however, had been enormous. Three house moves, three school moves for the children, and probably the most painful bit, the children hardly seeing their father, and Jo hardly seeing her husband.

It was not all work and not all separation though. One of our house moves saw us living in a small Mendip village a few miles south of Bristol. This village had a relatively young population, a lot of them our ages with children of similar age. We enjoyed a wonderful lifestyle making friends with many people. One of our sons, with obvious learning difficulties, was diagnosed as autistic at this time, an almost revolutionary diagnosis as autism was only just becoming widely recognised. This diagnosis allowed him to go to an excellent special needs school that saw his education advance enormously.

There was another side though. Being part of a wide group of friends meant taking part in a lot of 'men only' interaction, and I would often have great feelings of discomfort. Whilst I would always take part in the banter, crude jokes and robust behaviour with enthusiasm, the stress of feeling out of place would accumulate. It needed an outlet, and that outlet would result in an irrational display of anger, often with many others around, and often directed at Jo.

Despite this, we were very happy, but it was all to end. Another job move, another wrenching move to a new school for the children. It was not altogether my choice. The subsidiary I was working at was achieving healthy profits. It had not always been the case but as a team of dedicated managers, we had been able to save it and return it to profitability. The reward was to hear that it was now earmarked for closure by the divisional senior management. They had too many subsidiaries failing miserably and the distorted logic was that if they could take our successful business and merge it with a failure, then that failure would succeed. This may sound crazy logic, it most certainly was not mine, but it is the only logic that I could see behind such a move.

As always it was a promotion, a bigger job, and this time my job title was general manager. I inherited a job lot of small service centres that whilst being small, were managing to make big losses. Fortunately, I had also inherited a job with a lot of great people. All it needed was pulling together and making us into a team, and it was as a team that we turned the business around. This success, over two very hectic years, was noticed internally. It would be hard not to notice, we were the only ones not reporting staggering losses and, whilst our profits may have been modest, we showed what a well-motivated group of people with entrepreneurial spirit could achieve.

The constant travelling and working nearly impossible hours had substantially improved my income. Despite my often irrational behaviour, we were very happy. My sinful pride though was also still there. All this success was totally down to me. God was no longer in my life. I owed Him nothing. The gifts I had put to good use were all mine, nothing given to me. My pride was slowly destroying me but fortunately, I was to find in later years that the hand of Jesus had never moved away as my hand had done.

Our house was not totally devoid of thoughts of God. Jo had never lost her faith. She had, during the many periods of being left on her own, ventured to church but never found one that she could feel comfortable in, at least not comfortable enough to go into one on her own, an uncomfortable reminder to me of how much I had forsaken. Jo was going to need all of her faith soon though.

Although my small little part of this giant multinational was now making healthy profits the same could not be said for the rest of the organisation. It was clear that the huge losses being sustained by the group propped up with taxpayer subsidies, were unacceptable. I was beginning to become receptive to other offers of employment.

This was a huge time of change for British industry. Under the leadership of Margaret Thatcher state-owned enterprises were either being closed or sold off. I had made many contacts in business over the years and was seen as being successful. The inevitable invitation to 'have a chat' came and I found myself talking to a team of people who were managers of a subsidiary of a national undertaking, facing privatisation. It did not take me long to see the potential. This management team, unlike most of the rest, were not waiting to be taken over. They had the same urgency for business as me and needed a finance director to put together an employee buyout plan.

My existing job was secure, within the limitations of the overall security of the group, and this offer was full of uncertainty, but I had confidence in myself and my future fellow directors. Jo was greeted with the dreadful news of yet another house move being needed, something she found hard to accept, but as always, I was to go forward with her full support.

With some sadness, I handed in my notice to an organisation that had been my employer for ten years and then, with excitement started work for my new employers, a company that I had a significant ownership interest in. Six intensive months later, months often fraught with anxiety, and the buyout was done. It was not a management buyout though, we had chosen to make it an employee buyout, and anyone working for the company could have a share of its success.

The next two years were a whirlwind. We were the first of this organisation of 60 subsidiaries to be privatised. We soon set about acquiring others who did not approach the sell-off with the same degree of urgency that we did. Our company went from being one of the smallest to being the biggest on the block. Flotation on the stock market was inevitable and I was putting the necessary measures in place to prepare the groundwork. My pace of work was unsustainable, my diet dreadful, often rushing meals or eating a burger whilst dashing to my next appointment. The obsessional blindness prevented me from seeing what I was doing to myself.

It started with a pain behind my eye, then my eye and down my face, then in months it had become a crescendo of episodes of searing pain lasting hours at a time. It was becoming impossible to do my job. I sought medical help, and my GP referred me to a neurological consultant who admitted me to hospital for a barrage of tests.

After four weeks I left the hospital to be given the grim news. It was a condition called cluster headache; a little-understood neurological condition that produces episodes of pain considered to be amongst the most severe that the human body can inflict upon itself. Each episode lasted about two hours during which I would often be on the floor, banging my head and screaming in pain. Some days it would be relentless, episode following episode.

A very painful conversation followed with my colleagues. These attacks came on rapidly, without warning in less than five minutes. Apart from my own health making it impossible to continue they could not have a finance director prone to falling on his knees screaming, especially at this time in the company's progress, with stock market flotation looming. The finance director falling to his knees screaming when asked about future company profitability would not be a good look!

In all seriousness, it was painful for all. We had worked well, worked long and hard as a team, and now one of us was having to say goodbye. My colleagues were loyal and generous. When planning the employee buyout, I crafted the company articles to include a clause that only employees could be shareholders. My colleagues called an extraordinary general meeting of all shareholders to change that clause and allow me to keep my shareholding. With a stock market flotation in the near future this would guarantee my financial security. Not one shareholder opposed the proposal.

If my financial stability was now assured my mental stability was not. The psychological impact of such an abrupt cessation in a manic workaholic lifestyle was akin to an express train crashing into the buffers at one hundred miles per hour. Now, with time on my hands, space inside my brain to think, all those horrible thoughts of being out of step, different, not quite right, emerged. I needed something to do.

I had been referred to specialists at the National Neurological Hospital in London. There I was a guinea pig, trying out many different remedies still at the research stage. Sumatriptan, soon to be licensed as a drug to treat migraine, had shown promise, however, nothing could stop an attack once it had started. Speed was the key, at the very earliest signs it had to get into the bloodstream, so an auto-injector was developed. At the very first signs, you grab the injector, stab at the nearest available bit of exposed skin, feel the jab and hope for the best. The best was about a 50% success rate. The worst was supply, these things were expensive, and I was getting through more than the NHS could afford. With a limited supply and a limited success rate, I had at least something to fight back with.

Fighting the battle with my mind though was a different story. I had nothing to occupy it for all my waking hours. The doctors had told me to get more exercise, the last fifteen years of manic career progress had severely curtailed that aspect of my life. Jo jokingly referred to my old school atlas, which had lines drawn on a map between Lands' End and John O'Groats, the two points of the UK mainland furthest away from each other. I had drawn them when, in my teen years, a nuclear disarmament campaigner, Dr Barbara Moore, had walked the mammoth distance between the two points to raise awareness.

The seed was planted. Our house filled with ordnance survey maps, and I would spend hours with a map wheel charting different routes. Jo bravely suggested that she would accompany me, mostly out of concern for my health but also to rise to the challenge. One of our sons was co-opted to drive a motorhome as a support vehicle. Our route was meandering, over one thousand miles long, but avoiding as much as possible major roads and making as much use as possible of remote byways.

The first trip was an epic of what could go wrong would go wrong. Vehicle problems, driver navigation problems, unseasonably cold weather, and Jo with badly blistered feet were just some of the problems encountered on the way, without the almost daily attacks of cluster headaches. We finally arrived at John O'Groats, battered but triumphant. Of course, it was all my doing, nothing to do with God's blessings or Jo's bravery.

Coming home we stopped for dinner at a chain café in the far north of Scotland. A group of noisy children were in there. Their behaviour was different. In one of the most humbling moments of my life, the penny dropped. These children all suffered from Downs Syndrome and were on a rare trip out of their care centre, looked after by some dedicated people who put love before pride. If, at that moment I still kept God out of my life, I was made mindful of His grace to me.

We carried on home with me in a subdued mood. Back home I kicked myself for being so self-absorbed with my own personal problems that I was blind to all that I had been given. I made a proposal to my brave partner, let's do the return journey the following year, but not for us, to raise funds for kids not given the advantages that we had. Jo agreed. We would walk for a residential college providing support and education for severely disabled children, raising funds and awareness as we did.

Starting to plan the return journey also made me determined to take the fight against the cluster headaches. I was fed up with being told it was incurable, that for the rest of my life, I would have to live with episodes of unpredictable crippling pain. I was fed up taking medicines, some of which may not work, some, like Sumatriptan injections, would occasionally work, and some would try their best to kill me, as an overdose of Lithium had nearly done.

I looked at my last twenty years of lifestyle - a terrible diet, mostly some form of red meat and chips, and terribly sedentary. So much for that fit as a fiddle twenty-three-year-old. I now was an unfit puffing forty-three-year-old, with a self-destruct habit that I had started in my early teens that had increased dramatically during my pressure-cooker career years…smoking.

The sedentary bit I was doing something about, but could do far more. A diet of more vegetables and less red meat was started, and the biggest battle I have ever had in my whole life was confronted, the battle to give up smoking.

By the time we stood at the signpost at John O'Groats ready to start the thousand-mile trek Southwards, I was a non-smoker. Cluster headaches were still as bad as ever, but I was fitter and physically healthier. Six weeks later Jo and I arrived at Lands' End and a college for severely disabled kids had a few thousand pounds more in the bank. Jo, as brave as ever, had to endure terribly blistered feet, and we both had to endure awful weather. We started at John o' Groats in gale force winds, peaking at 70mph, and walking through England in the wettest June since records began. I was not surprised that on our arrival at Lands' End Jo could be heard muttering, 'Never again,' under her breath.

 A few more marathon walks followed, but on my own, Jo sensibly stayed at home. In my battle against cluster headaches, I had walked Lands' End to John O'Groats for the third time. I did not intend to, it was a misunderstanding at a talk I had given to one of our major sponsors, the local Lions Club. It had gone well, being held in the hospitality of a local bar and after the talk I had been asked if I would ever do it again. I mumbled something about, 'Never again,' but it seemed the questioner had heard differently. He was a reporter for the local rag, which the following week carried banner headlines of 'Marathon walker to do it again.' Fortunately, my son Steven was on hand to drive a support vehicle.

Another marathon walk that did not go quite so well was the hard and rugged Southwest Coast Path from Minehead in Somerset to Pool in Dorset. This encompassed the coastlines of Devon and Cornwall and 630 miles of some of the most wild and rugged headlands in England. A fall around the Lizard peninsular had left me battered, and bruised, with horribly swollen knees and cluster headaches, as bad as ever. By the time I reached Torquay, I was in constant pain and fifty miles later, just ninety miles from the end, with cluster headaches raging, I raised the white flag.

I was now considerably fitter and a few more organisations I was raising funds for were considerably richer. We were also richer. My colleagues had finished what I had started, the company was now a public one, and my holdings had increased substantially in value. Jo and I had never been in a position where we were free of debt and always worried about paying the bills. Now we were financially secure and relatively quite wealthy. If I did not recognise God in my life, He had not given up on me. We discussed our newfound wealth at length, deciding to share some of it with the family, and put a very large part of it into a charitable trust. We kept the trust anonymous; with it not bearing any of our names, but it was able, and continues to be able, to give meaningful donations to small local charities. This still left us financially secure but still needing to be careful.

I needed an occupation. I had always been interested in military history and wanted to travel to all those places that I had read about but now, with the opportunity, I could not find the tours I wanted. There was only one answer. Write my own tours.

For the next four years I travelled, wrote, researched, and travelled more. Cluster headaches were still a major problem, but I was continuing the battle. I still persisted in my new diet, and if anyone mentions fish, rice and salad today, expect me to politely decline dinner, for what had been my main diet for years. I was now physically quite fit and, most importantly, still a born-again non-smoker. I kept faithfully believing that one day it would pay off and I would be free of cluster headaches. I then received an invitation to a wedding. It was the other side of the world in Auckland, New Zealand.

I accepted the invitation with some trepidation. I knew the family involved to be hard-drinking farmers and if one thing was guaranteed to exacerbate cluster headaches, it was alcohol. I flew over, stopping for a few days in Fiji to allow my body to recover from jet lag. I then flew on to New Zealand, but not straight to Auckland, as I wanted my body to fully adjust to the time zones. I also wanted to recover from the journey well away from the wedding party guests, who I was sure would be partying well before the wedding. I stopped in a small town a few miles north of Auckland where I would be anonymous, giving myself five days of alcohol abstinence to recover.

That night, having survived an attack of cluster headaches earlier, I wearily went down to dinner. A disaster confronted me. It was someone's birthday. I never did find out who. A party was well underway, the alcohol flowing freely. Seeing a stranger in town, with typical Kiwi hospitality, a drink was sent over to my table. First one, then another, and then an invite to join the wedding party. Booze was the last thing I needed but a refusal would be rude, so I joined in. Apprehensively, I waited for the inevitable attack, the last of my self-injectors at the ready.

I had a headache the next morning, but not of the cluster type. In fact, I was puzzled. Apart from a rumble between the temples reminding me that I did not get to bed until 2 am, that morning I felt quite fresh, with no jet lag and more importantly, no cluster headaches. I did not know it then but that attack the previous afternoon was the last one I was to get. God had smiled upon me. Cluster headaches simply vanished from my life.

Returning home, I decided to expand my travels. One piece of history that has always fascinated me was the emigration of people across the USA in the nineteenth century. Emigrants tempted by land offers to travel from the overcrowded East Coast to the empty lands of the West, the so-called Oregon trails, and the later Gold Rush trails. American guidebooks at that time were sparse, so I had to do my own research, write my own guidebooks and in collaboration with a UK travel agent, organise my own tours. I received help from a huge number of organisations, mostly the Oregon State Tourist Authority and Oregon State University. I was pleased, in later years when it was time to move on, to gift the copyrights to the Oregon institutions.

I was now very busy, and it was to get busier. As I researched, my interest grew in the demographic changes in the United States at that period. The influx of people into the territories bordering the southern states had led to strains over slavery. This, and other factors, finally erupted into the war between the states, more commonly known as the American Civil War. This took me to the east side of the Mississippi, the southern states that formed the confederacy at that time, and to the University of Virginia. They became interested in my research and guidebooks and offered me a course of study, a PhD programme. More work, more obsessive absorption, I naturally said yes!

The end of my wanderings though was coming to an end. We had moved home, and this move required a basement-to-roof renovation of a large, sprawling, Edwardian rectory. In between flying backwards and forwards across the Atlantic, and working ridiculous hours in Virginia, I was getting increasingly busy at home. The small charitable foundation we had established was now getting very busy. The house was taking up a lot of time.

Adam, our autistic son, was displaying a lot of emotional and psychological problems, and whilst the internet was in its infancy, he was managing to spend more and more time in various chat rooms.

He was not the only one talking to people via the infant internet. I had involved myself with a number of other charities, as a volunteer, and one of those charities was a worldwide support network for adult survivors of abuse. I was the UK section leader, but a lot of the people I was engaging with as a support listener, were elsewhere in the world, and I was often working in the early hours of the morning.

Jo had also been busy. She was becoming more and more involved with the church that was just over the road from our house. She had been asked by an ex-neighbour if she could encourage a mutual friend to attend a Christian Alpha course being held at another friend's house in the village. Jo naturally agreed, but then asked, 'What about me? Could I come as well.' This brought her into contact with the local church who had warmly welcomed her into the congregation. We did not know it then, but God was laying the ground, introducing her to what was to prove a vital avenue of support for events that were about to unfold.

Jo and I both needed a break. We flew to St Lucia to spend a couple of weeks soaking up warm Caribbean sunshine. My father had been quite ill, but I had been assured that all would be well. Halfway through our break, we received news that my father had died.

We flew home. Jo contacted our sons to give them the news but there was no response from Adam. Time and again she left messages at his home, but no answer. Finally, the phone rang. In between torrents of abuse, Jo was able to discern that he was no longer in the country. He had developed a relationship with an American woman over the internet, she had visited just before we left for St Lucia, and whilst we were away, she had persuaded him to seek a new life in America. They had married in Las Vegas and were now in California.

It was devastating news to us both. We had met this woman; she was a lot older than our son, indeed we were to find out later that she was even older than me. She obviously liked the large house in eight acres of countryside that we owned. She certainly liked the large financial settlement we had given him, as well as the house he lived in, also given to him. He was wealthy but vulnerable. That vulnerability had been exploited.

I was emotionally exhausted. Numbly, with my sister, we organised my father's funeral. I read a eulogy to him. We were never super close, we argued a lot, but he was my dad, and he did his best for me. He had a bad time a few years earlier and I tried to be there for him. I just hoped that I had never hurt him like my son had hurt me.

It was a cold January, and shortly after the funeral, a couple of trustees of a charity nearby approached me to see if I would be the chair of trustees. They knew of my business past and needed a financially astute chairperson, and they knew of my role with adult survivors. This charity offered counselling services, to young and old, and it was doing excellent work from a run-down centre that they were having to leave anyway. I needed more work like I needed a hole in the head, but the emotional blows I had been hit with had weakened my mental resolve, and all those thoughts of being different were flooding back into my conscious mind. They had to be kept out and the only way I could keep them out was by either working or drinking.

I tried to keep in touch with Adam, and by June a reconciliation seemed possible. I flew over to California and met both of them in a hotel in Sacramento. I gritted my teeth and was incredibly nice. Two more visits and reconciliation was achieved. It was his life, nothing I could do about it, all we as parents wanted to achieve was to let him know that we were there if it all came crashing down.

My next visit brought the prospect of it all crashing down into focus. They greeted me with the news that they were buying a bit of land. Adam had a pilot's license for microlights, and he had converted that to an American license and was now going to open his own flying school. I questioned funding - were they taking a loan out, spreading the risk, secured against the freehold assets? No, he was putting all his eggs into one basket. I asked other questions, simple things like, 'I presume you have done a business plan,' only to be met by blank stares. I asked about insurance, and when told they couldn't get any, I wanted to crawl under the table. It was clear that they were going to invest everything they had in this venture, with no sharing of risk, no business plan, and no insurance in the most litigious country on the planet.

I flew back to London and spent a few days in my flat, pondering on the disaster unfolding. I had a number of flats in London. I first acquired one when I started flying transatlantic regularly. It was near Heathrow and was in a house converted into five flats, owned by two elderly couples. Shortly after buying one from one couple, I was approached by the other couple to see if I would buy one of theirs. I could see the writing on the wall. They both wanted to retire to the coast and by the end of two years, I was the sole owner of the house. All of the flats needed refurbishing, plus the infrastructure of the house itself. I acquired another flat in nearby Chiswick so I could have the house empty whilst refurbishments took place.

Jo had also been busy. She had become very involved with the church, hosting coffee mornings, supper evenings, Alpha courses and a lot more. Our house in Somerset had become almost an extension of the church. I did not mind. I quite liked it. I loved the church congregation; it was good to feel part of something. There were times I would curse my stupid pride as I watched from an upstairs window as Jo walked down our drive to go to church on Sundays, with me wishing that I could join her.

Then came another hammer blow. A call from California. There had been a flying accident, Adam's plane had crashed, and he had been flown to a specialist hospital in San Francisco for urgent surgery. We organised the first flight to San Francisco that we could get on. We arrived at the hospital to find Adam in intensive care after surgery. He had severely damaged both hands, they had been virtually severed, and it had taken 11 hours of surgery to save them.

His recovery was slow, and both Jo and I spent the next six months shuttling backwards and forwards to be what help we could. As far as his business was concerned that was ruined. There was no insurance to call upon.

By now a lot of people were beginning to get very concerned about my health. The toll of constant travelling, the commitments to so many charities, and the refurbishments both to our house in Somerset and the house in London, were draining me dry. There was also another problem.

Not everything was dry. I discovered my taste for wine all those years ago when I first sailed across the Atlantic. Over the years I had studied the subject and had a diploma, just one step below Master of Wine, but even though my diploma would have allowed me to study for the Institute of Masters of Wine, I declined. It was just too much, too serious and beyond my enjoyment zone. However, the house we had renovated had large cellars and I became a collector, a familiar face at London auctions.

Now I was not only collecting, but drinking, and the drinking was getting serious. Always a bottle with dinner and often a bottle afterwards. Sometimes, if I was due to take a late call from my adult survivors' group, then it would be a bottle by my computer.

Chapter 4
Finding God, Breaking down

It was clear to everyone but me that I had too many commitments, was pursuing too many goals, and simply was not looking after myself. I didn't care. I was now an emotional wreck inside. I did not fit in anywhere, success meant nothing if you could not rid yourself of that need to always have to prove who you are. I was just plodding through one day after another. Clearly, a crisis was looming, and I was about to crash into some form of physical or mental breakdown, but before it happened, I was to get some help. Jesus was there with the Light even if I was keeping the door firmly closed.

It was a bright July day. Jo had planned a church social gathering that evening. The weather forecast had promised all sorts of gloom and doom but for once the forecasts were wrong. About thirty people were gathered on our rear terrace overlooking the beautiful Somerset countryside in lovely late evening sunshine. The air was full of birdsong. I was trying my best to be a genial host, pouring drinks and indulging uncomfortably in small talk. One of the church leaders came wandering over to me. 'How are you David'? he asked, then having been given the usual, 'Great, wonderful, spiffing, couldn't be better,' he looked me in the eye and casually asked, 'Would you like to give yourself to Jesus?' Holding his gaze the words came out of my mouth without any thought whatsoever, 'Yes, I would.'

I would like to say that fanfares were heard, fireworks shot into the night sky and the earth trembled in joyous acclamation but there was none of that. I had opened the door to God again, I had let the light of Jesus in, and inside there was just peace.

Outside there was no peace. I had so overcommitted that I was working flat out from seven in the morning to seven at night when I would then just collapse over a glass of wine. The phone ringing was sometimes relentless, and the travel was a constant. All this against a backdrop of sheer emotional exhaustion from the events of the last few years.

I started to worship, not just at our home in Somerset, but also in Chiswick. I was walking home from the train station one evening, and it was a gorgeous early August summer evening. I had been recommended a restaurant and as I walked up a side street looking for it, I heard the sound of worship. I followed the sound to what looked like a community hall. The sound was the worship band of a local church practising. It was loud, it was vibrant, it was uplifting, and it was a signal to me that I had found my church. I might not have found the restaurant that I was looking for, but I was to be fed in other ways.

It was Christian, Protestant but not Anglican, and quite different to what I had been used to. Some aspects made me uncomfortable; I would describe it almost as Christian fundamentalist, but it was happy and I could sing my praises to the Lord, my lousy voice drowned out by the music from the exuberant band. I look back now and realise that God, knowing what was coming, ensured that I had the strength and love of Jesus all around me.

The summer went by, autumn came, and I was in London overseeing yet another project, an extension to my house to make one flat bigger. It was a cold damp building site that I was overnighting in, a night in my warm comfortable flat in Chiswick being discarded in favour of being here first thing in the morning. The heating boiler had given up the ghost, and the damp smell of builder's rubble hung in the air. All I wanted to do was sleep but instead, I sat on the edge of the bed, staring at a mirror on the wall in despair. I was just praying, pleading, 'Father, what is wrong with me, what is it inside that causes me to constantly commit to keeping busy, why can I never have peace, why do I always feel so much unease?'

I don't know whether it was for a few seconds or a few minutes. I was looking at my reflection in that mirror, even I had to admit I looked like a tired haggard mess, then the reflection changed. It was still me but at the same time not me. The hair was longer, the skin smoother, the features softer. I was looking at the image of a female, but it was still me.

I was in shock. It was as though a wall had fallen down in front of me. Nearly fifty years of internal churning had been explained. I was the wrong way around. Suddenly it all made sense, but it was horrific sense. The feelings running through me must have paralleled the feelings of that child all those years ago, the child that woke from a happy pleasant dream to all those feelings of shame and embarrassment for he had been a girl in those dreams.

The next day I tried to brush it away. I met with my builders, agreed to some revised plans and returned to my flat in Chiswick. In the past, the response to thoughts like I had the previous night, would result in an explosion of manic macho activity. This time I simply was not strong enough. Well, again that pride. Was it I was not strong enough or was it that someone was steering me to a resolution I simply could not have dreamed of?

Over the next few weeks, the desire to see myself in female form grew to be overwhelming. At first, I visited a transvestite dressing agency for a makeover but there was something wrong both with the look and the social community I found myself in. We had totally different motivations. I would much prefer to look like Miss Marple than I would a caricature of Miss World.

I then found another agency specializing in producing the 'natural look.' It was run by a lovely lady called Julie who seemed to understand my inner conflict and who appreciated the need to tone everything down. I was embarrassed, ashamed, and disgusted with myself but also had an irresistible need. This lady used to work on the costume drama sets of the BBC and knew what transformation was all about.

I stared into the mirror as the make-up was being applied, half feeling like Coco the Clown, half feeling very embarrassed. Julie asked if I had thought of a feminine name. I explained I had never done anything like this before, and never even thought about it, in fact, I had held a lot of transphobic beliefs. I did recall those dreams of troubled boyhood, that girl, whose name was Jennifer, but absolutely nothing since then.

When she finished the make-up, she asked me to close my eyes as the hair was put in place. I had not yet had the experience of hair spray in the eyes! I could feel it being fitted, combed into shape, and was then asked to open my eyes. The effect was electrifying. Staring back at me in the mirror was the person that deep in my subconscious mind I always knew I was. All those defences I had put up to avoid looking for the cause of that internal agitation were broken, gone forever. There was no turning back.

I asked where I could acquire the same hair. Julie came back with the box it had been packed in. Looking at the label, she announced that the manufacturer was Rene of Paris, and the style was called 'Jennifer.' The coincidence was too much. Jennifer had met Jennifer and the name had been chosen.

I returned to my flat, my mind was in turmoil. Clearly, when I had looked at that reflection in the mirror something had happened inside me, but I was a bloke, why on earth did I want to see myself as a woman? I fought against all that had happened, concluded that it all was just a sleazy, unnatural bit of escapism, and went to the pub.

The sleazy, unnatural bit of escapism would not go away though. The genie was out of the bottle. Now the guilt of deceit would start to enter my troubled mind. The feelings inside grew and grew. I started to acquire a wardrobe and I joined an internet chat room as a transvestite called Jenny. I felt so uncomfortable with the attention that the transvestite designation attracted that I changed my identity and the shortened form of my name, calling myself Jenni. This was all being done in secret, without Jo or any of my friends knowing. The feelings of deceit were now compounding the anguish inside but as I sank into an identity crisis, the ability to relate to others, even someone as close to me as Jo, started to diminish. I was now suffering massive confusion inside so how could I relate to someone something that I could not understand himself?

I needed somewhere to keep Jenni's wardrobe; and a friend offered me a short-term lease on a small, one-bedroom basement flat near my Chiswick flat. As much as I felt ashamed and revolted at my behaviour and the world of deceit I was entering, the need to embrace the female persona, now known as Jenni grew and grew. Friends from my online chat room came over for dinner. It was the first time I had ever met anyone else as Jenni, except for Julie who had first helped me to see her.

A month later those same friends took me to a fetish fair. That evening, returning home, we all stopped for dinner just around the corner from the tiny basement flat. This was the first time that I, as Jenni, had been out in a perfectly normal mainstream social environment. As my nerves settled, as I realized that everyone else in the restaurant was just continuing as normal and not staring in shock, disgust or amusement at me, something happened. I felt content. Gone was that internal churning agitation that had been part of me for the whole of my life. Gone was that feeling of inadequacy, of being different, of being not in step with everyone else. Even though I knew that to most people, including myself, I looked a freak, a joke, a bloke in a frock, despite all those things, for the first time in my whole life I felt normal.

The pressure within to live as a female was inexorable, but so, too, was the anguish it was causing. I was a man, but when I presented as one, my life was one of churning turmoil. When I presented as a female, there was peace and calm inside. However, there was also a self-disgust at indulging in a sleazy, unnatural activity and self-disgust at the growing deceit, especially the distancing it was causing between me and Jo. It was coming up to nearly a year since Jenni had first manifested herself in me and now, she was taking over my life. I had to stop it. I did.

Over the next few months, the internal pain was unbearable. I could no longer survive just living as a man, but I could not return to that sleazy life of living as a female, living in a world of secrecy and deceit. My relationship with Jo was falling apart as the internal churning agitation would make me volatile and unpredictable. The slightest disagreement with her would see me storming off back to my London home, leaving Jo becoming more and more certain he was sharing his life with another woman.

Just as it was as a child, I could no longer associate with society, and being with large groups of people would cause me to become almost hysterical and seek solitude elsewhere. At a meal with most of Jo's family present, I had upset everyone by abruptly getting up and leaving the restaurant, as the need to be alone, to find isolation, overwhelmed me. Enjoying a short break with Jo caravanning in the Shropshire countryside, I had repeatedly stormed off late at night to spend hours sitting somewhere in the middle of nowhere, isolated and alone, with the screaming pain and anguish inside.

My ability to worship was also suffering at my Chiswick church. I felt sure that any revelation of gender variance would result in immediate expulsion from the church, at the very least. I could no longer attend; I could not live a lie in a house of God, so I stopped going. However, I might have left the church, but I was soon to discover that God had not left me and that Jesus had a very strong grip on my hand.

I had been experiencing wave after wave of compulsion to destroy myself. On one occasion, I found myself at Hammersmith underground station. Having just missed a train I knew it was going to be a little wait before another one arrived. Before another train came in I could do it, my eyes, looking down at the rails became transfixed, especially at the live rail. My toes were literally over the platform edge, my body rocking, staring at those rails, at that live rail that was just half a second away from releasing me into the blackness of death, releasing me from the pain and turmoil that was tearing me apart.

I felt someone grip my right arm. As I tried to spin around to see who it was, so my legs started moving me backwards. It was as if I had no control over my movements, no control over which direction I faced or where I went. My legs had a mind of their own as I walked sideways, backwards from that platform. Finally, whoever it was let go of their grip. I had control of my legs again; I spun around to confront whoever it was that had interfered and there was no one. Instead, I was staring at an exit sign. I took the hint, walked up the stairs and walked home in the pouring rain. As I turned left to go up the side of the beautiful Christ Church Turnham Green, I noticed the words on the banner adorning the railings. It was from Acts. 'Believe in the Lord Jesus and you will be saved.'

'Believe in the Lord Jesus.' How those words hit home. How I cursed my weakness of faith. It was not depression causing me to be suicidal. Just as it was when I was a child, it was the knowledge that I did not belong. I was not a man, and neither could I live as a woman. Unable to associate or identify with society, there was no place for me, no reason to be here, no identity to strive for to keep alive.

I knew that mentally I was falling apart. I also felt shaken by what I now saw as an act of rebellion against my faith. God gave me this life, God gave me this beautiful world to live in, God gave me the beautiful person that was my Jo, someone who would be devastated if I were to take my own life. If God wanted me to end my life, then I would no longer be here. Clearly, He didn't. My faith once more became my backbone. 'Believe in the Lord Jesus,' that same belief that as a child kept me so safe.

I knew I had to seek help. I asked around and obtained a referral to a renowned London clinic specializing in treating mental and psychological illnesses. Ironically, it was the same clinic that had cared for me when I was a child.

I turned up with a garbled story about being depressed but not revealing the most important part due to the deep shame I felt within. The doctors immediately recognized a mental state close to breakdown and urged me to accept admittance into a place of safety. This I could not do; it would mean my secret world being exposed. The specialists in the first instance diagnosed a form of post-traumatic stress disorder, an accumulation of stresses going as far back as that tragic accident on the cliffs of Ben Nevis, exacerbated by that sudden and traumatic health breakdown that caused early retirement. As they started to chart my life history, a pattern of very contrasting peaks and troughs began to emerge. They listened as I described how I always felt the need to run through life at 120 miles an hour and questioned what I could be running from.

They questioned whether I had repressed sexual problems and concluded I was comfortable as a heterosexual male. What I was not comfortable with was where all this was leading. In the last few weeks, I had returned to secretly living and dressing as Jenni again. My mind could no longer bear not having the release of peace and calm I felt when I was presenting as female.

I was being cornered. It was time to overcome the shame and self-loathing and explain this sleazy desire I had to be female to the psychotherapists; how I was dressing in secret as a female and how I felt no longer able to exist in society presenting as a male. It was to them as though someone had turned the lights on.

Over the next few appointments, they started to rebuild my childhood. Bit by bit, working on known instances and dates, they saw the same pattern emerge that was now apparent in the adult they were treating. Childhood gender dysphoria was indicated in almost every incident. They explained to me that, in their opinion, I was suffering from gender dysphoria. They explained how it had nothing to do with sexuality or how we are physically made, it is how our minds, our brains perceive ourselves to be and how the conflict caused by being of one gender, but having to live in the other, creates the deep unhappiness I had been experiencing.

It was all getting a bit heavy. I was relieved to hear it was a medical condition, not a mental or psychological one but then they spoilt it all by telling me that it can cause very severe psychological distress that could result in mental breakdowns. They also explained that no one really had any idea what causes it, but an accepted theory is that it is partly caused by a chemical screw-up in the brain at about 16 weeks into gestation. This is when there is a burst of hormonal activity that is thought to tell the developing fetal brain whether it is in a female or male body.

All good theory but where do I go from here? They referred me to a specialist in Gender Dysphoria. They talked about permanent changes. I just wanted to get out of there. I agreed I would see a gender specialist at the earliest opportunity and until then, I would remain under their close care. I never made that appointment and neither did I go back. For me, it was akin to a death sentence. There was no way that I could even contemplate being able to ever live and be accepted as a trans-woman. It was fine in theory to talk about my gender being at variance to my body and counter to the way I was raised and lived all my life. The practicality was that it simply could not be resolved.

Jo was going through hell. Having stood by me through the worst years of my life she was being treated like rubbish by me. It was not intentional but that does not ease in any way what she was going through. She was certain that I had another woman, strange parcels kept turning up addressed to someone called Jenni Brown. My behaviour was volatile, erratic, rude and cruel. It was her faith that kept her going, and her prayers to our Father God, she was even resorting to writing letters to Him. I wished I could tell her, I screamed for a way, but the words could not be strung together.

I think for both of us we can say that these were the worst times we have ever spent together. It was an emotional stand-off. I wanted to tell her everything but could not think of a way to even start. She wanted to ask but did not wish to strain further an already volatile relationship. How we both prayed for our Father God to show us the way. How weak was my faith that I could not see it was Jesus showing me the way, guiding me, holding me when darkness enveloped me and guiding me towards a brilliant light?

I returned to my little basement flat, Jenni's secret home. Curled up on the settee, I agonized over my predicament. I now knew that all those specialists were right. This was not a piece of escapism that would disappear as my exhausted mind recovered. This was real. I had a serious gender problem and desperately needed help. As the night wore on, so my distress grew. In the solitude of my basement flat I started to think of the unthinkable, a future without Jo. This plunged me into a greater and deeper spiral of despair. I prayed and prayed for guidance. That night, my tortured mind whirled. Sleep was sporadic. I drifted through the night in a zombie-like state; hardly aware of what I was doing.

The following morning, I struggled to motivate myself into some form of normal existence, The night before became just a blur, a bewildering and confused memory of a night where it was impossible to tell what had been real and what had been a nightmare punctuating a tortured sleep. I had made arrangements that evening to meet a friend for dinner, someone who, like me, had experienced post-traumatic stress disorder. It was mutual support for each other. I got through the day and enjoyed an evening in the company of my friend. Returning to my basement flat, I was aware that I had been without my mobile phone and had not been able to ring Jo, something I did every evening normally without fail. There might have been unendurable tension between us at this time, but we still felt that need to talk to each other.

I switched on my mobile and saw the 'messages waiting' alert. The first was a message from Jo, asking what the hell the message left on my mobile answering service was all about. The next was from my secretary, pleading to know where I was. The next was from Jo again, basically saying, 'David, please get in touch.' The next was again from my secretary saying she was with Jo driving to London, please get in touch. The last two messages were strident pleas from Jo, saying she was at their London flat, please, please get in touch, then a WPC from the local police station asking me to get in touch with the police.

My mind whirled. The calls all related to something left as the answer phone greeting on my mobile, but whilst the events of the night before were a memory of deep distress and despair, the specifics of those memories were vague and hazy, having been wiped out by a brain that really did not want to go there. I tried to access the greeting. My hands were shaking, my mind barely functioning, and in an almost panicky rush to listen to the message, I deleted it. I was never to hear what had been left.

I called Jo. She almost screamed at me to come home, then explained the content of the message I had left as a greeting. It was a two-minute monosyllabic drone, basically saying goodbye to those I loved. Jo had heard it and confided in the local parish priest, who shared her view that it was deeply distressing and not just a cry for help, it conveyed real intent. Jo had then turned to my secretary, someone who probably, outside of my immediate family, knew the workings of my mind more than anyone. She concurred with the priest; this was not the David she knew; this was gravely serious. Together, she and Jo had set off straight away to come and find me. Arriving at our London flat they found no trace of me there, which was not surprising as I had spent the last two nights in Jenni's secret basement flat. In desperation, they contacted the police, who on hearing the answering message concurred this was serious and immediately posted me as an at-risk missing person.

I then spoke to one of the two policewomen who had first interviewed Jo. They asked where I was and whether I could meet them at the local police station. I had to smile. My flat was literally just across the little road that ran up the outside of the police station. I wandered over and met with the WPC. She casually asked where my car was. It was a distinctive Jaguar sports car, bright red with a personalised number plate. Quite easy to spot but no one had spotted it. I simply stared at the bright red car she stood next to. Her eyes followed my gaze, she looked at the personalised number plate, saying nothing she invited me inside. Well, I did have a valuable and desirable car, so where was the safest place to park it if not outside the opposite police station!

We went inside to an interview room. She exhorted me to allow them to take me to a place of safety, a hospital where I could be cared for, a nice way of threatening me with being sectioned. I screamed inside to say yes, there was nothing I wanted more than to be released from this pain, but then the secret would be out. The decision I had to make but couldn't face would be made for me, and I wanted it to be in my own time, not someone else's. I had to say no and asked to be returned to Jo and my secretary. It was not that easy. The police had a duty of care. Their first responsibility was for me to be safe even if that meant having me admitted to a place of safety against my will. They talked to Jo and my secretary, talked to the hospital, weighed up all the pros and cons and finally agreed to release me into Jo's custody.

Reunited with Jo we returned home. The end of the whole nightmare had begun. Jo now knew that there was a terrible conflict inside me. I knew it was only a matter of time before the source of that conflict would be divulged. I was not yet ready, but the key had been placed into the lock. I held on to those words, 'Believe in the Lord Jesus.' Who, after all, had guided me to leave a message, a message I was destined never to hear but a message that alerted those so dear to me that an awful conflict was tearing me apart.

A few days later the opportunity to turn that key came from an unexpected source. Jo's mum, at the age of 81, had decided she was going to see Australia, to go to the wedding of her grand-niece, and to stop with a niece she had not seen for many years. Whilst stopping with her niece, she learned of a family secret. Jo's uncle, her mum's brother, had been a closet transvestite for most of his life. On her return to England, she confided in Jo, who immediately sprung to her uncle's defence. 'What harm has it done?' she asked; 'Who has he hurt? If it brings him happiness, then good for him, and just whose business is it, anyway?

To me, it was like hearing the key start to turn in the lock. Time and time again, in after-dinner discussions, I would return to the subject of Jo's uncle and family reaction. Finally, one evening the conversation took the right course. I was unusually relaxed that evening; Jo, too, had felt more relaxed and more willing to step on thorny ground. She asked an innocent question, anticipating a sharp retort from the most non-effeminate, macho man she knew. 'Have you ever thought or been tempted to cross-dress' she asked, smiling. The response was not what she expected.

I told her the whole story, explaining what gender dysphoria was, how I now had an appointment to see a gender specialist, and how I had been warned that my only hope to return to a normal life was to transition from being male to being female. For two hours Jo listened as her whole life was being turned upside down. As she listened, the consequences for her became apparent. This quiet, reserved woman had no reservations despite the awful consequences for her. She saw her life was with the person she had married. She wanted him well, even if that meant he was now she.

She got up, walked around the table, put her arms around me and quietly muttered the words, 'I would rather have a living sister than a dead husband.' God's love had truly smiled upon us. Thanks to the strength He had given us we were together and stepping into an unknown future together.

Chapter 5
Transition

It was not a done deal. For both of us, there was a lot of uncertainty. Jo had been through a couple of years of hell living with me and there was no way she could commit to continuing to live a life with someone who had treated her so badly. Knowing the cause was a relief, there was another woman involved, but that woman was her husband. She now had insight into the terrible difficulties her husband had faced, but what would the consequences be, how would she cope?

For me there was a relief it was in the open, the deceit had ended, and I still had Jo in my life. What was the future though? To look at me, still very much a bloke, and to think of what all the specialists were saying, what my own mind was saying, was like looking into an inky blackness. It simply seemed inconceivable that my outward physical appearance and presentation could ever meet what my mind wanted.

For both of us, we had to have an answer to, 'How will it end.' The first step was for Jo to at least meet the work in progress that I called Jenni. First, it was seeing me with lipstick on, a bizarre sight, the macho man with beard stubble on his face and Max Factor's finest all over his lips. We then moved on to a brief flirtation with me wearing a wig. Slowly, we inched towards that first time that Jenni would introduce herself to Jo. We had decided that our first meeting would be in a restaurant near my no-longer secret flat in London opposite the police station.

I don't know what went wrong that night. We had travelled to London together and had stayed together at our London flat, but then I had taken myself off to Jenni's basement to get myself ready for the evening. I was dreadfully nervous about this; the first time Jo was to meet Jenni. Everything I had meant to wear, mostly the most demure clothes in my wardrobe, somehow seemed out of place. I ended up putting on a most awful bright red skirt, something bought for 99 pence on eBay, something that finished well above my knees, shiny stockings, a black tarty top that wouldn't quite button up properly, showing off liberal amounts of my male beer belly and all worn underneath a wig that resembled something belonging to a mid-1960s teenager. I looked dreadful. That first meeting was a restrained and difficult affair, Jo wondering just who this caricature of a 1970s tart was.

Either way, it was a disaster. The following morning saw Jo rifling through my wardrobe, throwing most of the contents into a pile, whilst snorting with a mixture of disgust and amusement, before finding something that looked almost half decent. Finally, she threw some things at me, told me to put those on and then dragged me off to go to Marks and Spencer's for a bit of clothes shopping.

We needed to know what the future held, and I was still sitting on the fence. I continued to see the psychotherapist I had turned to, at the end of that dreadful period of emergence, the person who more than anyone kept me sane through that period and was to be my rock through transition. He had meticulously broken down the conflicting walls inside - David who loathed Jenni and Jenni who wanted rid of her jailer, to finally rebuild both as one person. A person beginning to feel strong again, being able to emerge from that desperately dark tunnel. Even so, I still fought hard to keep that feeling of masculinity; something so hard fought for as I emerged from childhood into adulthood, was not going to be given up easily.

Jo was seeing a consultant psychotherapist at a Gender Identity Clinic nearby. He had offered Jo emotional support. Yet again we also were to find that God had intervened. The psychotherapist could have been anything, but as he introduced himself to her, he confided, 'I am an ordained priest in the Anglican church. Is this acceptable to you?' The comfort of being able to broach such a sensitive and personal subject with someone who shared her faith was an incredible lifeline for her, and again a reminder that faith was the rock that we could depend upon. He listened to Jo describe the terrible story of her life in recent years and professed huge admiration for her courage and fortitude, in the face of a catalogue of disasters and relationship difficulties that would have broken many. He finally, over the next few weeks, reached a point where felt he needed to talk to me if he was to be able to help Jo further.

With Jo's permission, he agreed to talk to me, something I welcomed. This would be the first time that Jo and I would be able to bare our souls collectively to someone, who was not only a highly respected consultant, but someone who also possessed huge humanitarian values and beliefs. He listened to my history, a synopsis of all that had gone on before, and agreed with everyone else, yes it was gender dysphoria, it was primary, meaning I was born with the condition and the symptoms were there as a child before the onset of puberty. He also recognized that I had an intense need now to just move on, to step forward from the denial, accept who and what I was and begin the process of rebuilding my life, our lives, on a solid foundation and not on the shifting sands of trying to be something I wasn't.

This man never brought faith into the discussion but for me, it was the most important part of my discussion. Like most Christians I was aware of biblical passages such as Deuteronomy 22:5. Even though I had felt the steadying hand of God throughout the worst moments, indeed thinking back to that incident at Hammersmith station, it was that steady hand that had a firm grip on my arm, I was still plagued by thoughts that I was offending God. This man, with his simple humanity, eased those worries. I was born with Gender Dysphoria, it was neither fetish nor sexual deviation, I was struggling with how I was made. He also reassured me of God's unwavering love, that God would love both of me regardless.

By sharing with this incredible man my innermost fears in front of Jo, I could see more clearly than ever that I just had to come off the fence. The need to live as one person was unavoidable. The need to just be Jenni was obvious. The need to accept whatever diagnosis was made and stick to that decision with focused discipline was paramount.

It was time for no more ambiguity. More and more, the times I was retreating to being David were causing great internal torment, resulting in bouts of petulant tantrums that were beginning to wear down Jo. This consultant agreed and made the necessary arrangements to send me for one more referral, to one of the most eminent specialist psychiatrists in the country.

The day arrived. It was just over four months since I had first told Jo about my feminine persona. I was sitting with this specialist who spoke with great calm authority, who knew, had seen many times before, people with the same stresses as me. He had interviewed me for a couple of hours and referred to the very copious historical notes that travelled with me. He concluded there was no doubt whatsoever that I had gender dysphoria, and it was a primary condition. All my previous assertions that it was only fantasy were debunked by this specialist, who had pointed out all the evidence from childhood onwards that had been apparent long before those final traumatic events that had driven David to the edge and allowed my prison walls to come tumbling down.

He now turned to my current situation of trying to live in limbo. He asked whether it was fair on Jo to keep this limbo going. She had been devastated by my erratic behaviour during the period of emergence, and further devastated by hearing that I was gender dysphoric and would have to undergo changes. The least she deserved now was a stable platform to move forward on. For myself, how long did I want to keep beating myself up? The very happiness and contentment I feel when presenting myself in my true psychological identity of female surely says everything when compared to that anguished frantic male rushing around at 120 miles an hour. In summary, his words were, 'You are now Jennifer; there is no way back. Yes, it's tough, life is tough, deal with it.'

His words hit home. I accepted his diagnosis. I accepted I would start the process of medically supervised transition under his care and direction. There would now be no turning back. I came home to Jo. We sat and talked. She now knew the worst but also knew what we had to do to get over the worst. Our love for each other made us inseparable and we knew where that love had come from. It was time to rally support and start to tell people, starting with our church family.

Transition can be hell. It is a time when the full brunt of ignorance, bigotry and prejudice will hit right in the face. A time when just going out to do the normal everyday things will be a time of apprehension, of not knowing if this is going to be the day to be sneered or jeered at, backs turned, spat at, verbally assaulted, physically threatened or become a victim of a hate crime. To start that process was like walking off the edge of a cliff.

We started to tell our church family individually, couple by couple. I was so apprehensive, how on earth could they possibly accept that this most masculine of men would be turning up as she? All we got back was love, total unconditional love. Time and time again, a couple, individual or small group, would listen with disbelief, sometimes incomprehension, then stand and give us both a warm, loving hug.

I also needed a church. I had ceased going to the church I went to as David, I would never in a million years have been accepted as Jenni. I was spending most of the time in my London flat and was without somewhere to worship feeling desperately lonely. Just over the road from my flat was the beautiful Christ Church Turnham Green, an Anglican church, but from reputation, quite conservative. Apart from one hugely apprehensive visit to Sainsbury's, I had not yet stepped foot outside of my door, in daylight and alone, as Jenni. It was time to meet Anglican conservatism full in the face.

I walked into the 9 am service and instead met love full in the face. The service was led by a lady lay preacher who went out of her way to come over and say hello. Seeing a strange face, in fact, a very strange face, in the congregation, others came over with a warm welcome. The churchwarden introduced himself. I can remember that sermon even today. It was from Acts 12. The Holy Spirit also introduced himself. As always when I felt so much of the love of our Lord carried through his Spirit, the tears would involuntarily flow down my face. Many asked what was wrong, I had to explain they were tears of joy. I came home after the service finished, had a cup of tea, my head spinning with all that had happened, and went back for the 11 am service. Christ Church Turnham Green was to prove to be my rock.

Jo and I continued to grow stronger together. With the strength of the love that we had been shown, we moved forward to tell others, and slowly but surely all the world we knew came to know Jenni. I was truly blessed, acceptance and love, rather than rejection and hostility was everywhere.

Obviously where it would all end was occupying our minds. As more and more of my life became her, rather than him, so physical transition became not only inevitable but imperative. I felt that I was living a lie.

I started facial depilation, a process to remove my beard. There are two main techniques; electrolysis, where a fine needle is inserted into the hair follicle and a high voltage charge sent down it, or laser, intense pulsed light techniques, where intense light is absorbed by the hair follicle, which is then basically burnt away. Whichever procedure is opted for, there is one truth for both; it hurts, and even using the quicker technique it was going to be 15 months of pain before my beard finally went, during which at one time putting lipstick on was agony for two weeks after having half my lip burnt and blistered by the laser.

I was placed on hormone therapy from the beginning. A female brain in a male body awash with testosterone is bad enough, a female brain in a male body trying to become female is impossible to live with. As testosterone production was repressed and estrogen took its place, so a peace came about; yet more freedom from that nagging anguish; yet a further step towards feeling complete and whole.

Of great issue was my voice. It was not particularly deep for a male but had loads of chesty resonance. I was often complimented on having a nice speaking voice, but now, dressed as a woman, sounding like a bloke with a nice speaking voice, it was most definitely an unwelcome attribute. It is probably my greatest failure. There is a surgical procedure to raise the voice by an octave or so but that all went to pot when another surgery, and insertion of an intubation tube, broke a load of stitches and sent me back to square one. I also underwent a lot of training to change my vocal intonation but gave up when I realised all that was doing was making me sound like a drag queen. I opted to just accept that I had a deep voice.

Holding the pitch is difficult in stressful situations. Under stress, the throat tends to tighten up and the voice slips down a few octaves exaggerating that bass resonance typical of a male. Driving to London one day, in the days when I still had my pose-mobile, a bright red Jaguar sports convertible with a three-digit personalised number plate, I was pulled over by a policeman.

Coming to the passenger side of my vehicle, he opened the door and started to give me the nicest telling-off I have ever had. Apparently, I had committed a slight infringement of the speed limit, not sufficient to warrant a ticket being issued but enough for him to want to pull me over and correct me on my driving. I couldn't help thinking this was a nice way of saying, 'I'm bored and wanted to see who the smartly dressed bit of totty was driving the posh car with the personalised number plate.'

Focusing intently on giving me a professional assessment of my driving skills he finally asked some details, namely name and where I was going to. I flashed my eyelids, gave him my 'oh so demure damsel in distress' look, shyly lowered my eyes and through my constricted voice box said, 'My name is Jennifer, officer, and I'm on my way to a dinner engagement in London.' The voice did not match the rest of the package. I might just as well have said, 'Me name's Dave, mate, and I'm on my way into town to have a few pints with me mates.' The policeman stared. The look said it all. He mumbled something about driving more carefully in future and sped off in his car. Meanwhile, the smartly dressed bit of totty was looking in her vanity mirror stroking her chin and contemplating whether she needed a shave that night before going out.

Despite the voice, I also returned as a volunteer with the Samaritans. I had first been one many years back but then my own needs became so pressing, I was incapable of offering emotional support to anyone. An organisation offering emotional support to the despairing and suicidal, mostly through telephone contact, might seem a strange choice for someone having difficulty with their voice. However, it was almost a necessity, a calling for me to do so, it was not only giving something back to those who had given something to me, it was being there for the next David, the next confused, bewildered, hurt, despairing person who just needed a friendly, non-judgmental and unprejudiced person to talk to. Every time I went on duty and spoke to someone like that, I felt privileged to be the one who answered that phone.

After that incident with the policeman, I faced the next imperative, changing my legal documents. My driver's license was changed to tell the traffic police I was a female driver, my tax records were changed so I could pay tax as a female citizen of the state, and my medical records were changed to record the fact I was now female.

The big day though was the day I went to collect my new passport. My appointment was for 12 o'clock and after queuing for just 10 minutes outside, just before noon, I was allowed into the building. Having cleared security, I nervously waited to be called. I didn't wait long; then, even more nervously, I made my way to the counter; A very helpful official checked all my documents before disappearing into a huddle with his colleague. His colleague, a lovely smiling lady came over after a few minutes and said, 'OK Miss Brown, take this voucher to the cash desk, pay the fee, and exactly four hours after that, you can collect your new passport.'

I collected my receipt with the time stamp on it and had four hours to kill, so I dashed off to Oxford Street to have my ears pierced. He had only pierced one ear when my phone rang. Something told me it was the passport office, 'Do you mind?' I asked, giving the piercing man no choice as I got out of the chair and rushed to my bag to retrieve my phone. It was the passport office. They had forgotten to ask for me to leave my birth certificate, 'Be right back,' I shouted to the astonished piercing man. I dashed out and hastily flagged down a taxi to take me back to the passport office, one ear pierced and the other still with a bit of tape attached to it.

Security clearly had some sympathy with the breathless woman with one pierced ear, and cleared me to go to the counter straight away. The same lovely smiling woman took my birth certificate. 'Everything seems OK - the same time as on your receipt, possibly a few minutes late.' A dash back to Oxford Street, muttered apologies to the piercing man, who seemed to pierce my other ear with quite a sadistic grin on his face, then back to wait in the collection area. Finally, my name was called, 'Miss Brown to Position 2.'

'Can you check the details please Ma'am?' said the woman. I looked only at one line. 'Yes, that's ok' I said, handing my passport back. She looked at me a little quizzically before handing it back to me, 'I mean can you take a few minutes and check all the details?' she asked. 'That's OK,' I said handing it back. She started to hand it back to me again, noticed the tears streaming down my face, and softly read all the details back to me. I nodded my confirmation they were all correct. 'Are you OK?' she asked with gentle concern. 'Yes, it's just that one line means so much to me,' I sniffled back. 'Oh, what line is that?' she asked, 'The line where it says 'Sex' and then has an 'F' against it,' I blubbered. She smiled, understood what I had been saying and handed me my nice shiny new passport with the words, 'Welcome to the start of your new life, Miss Brown.' So lovely, they all were, the passport office, all the way through from my original telephone call to discussing procedure, they showed a kindness and compassion rare in so many places. Thank you all.

Life was becoming quite normal, but the passage to normality for anyone travelling the route that I was on, was not without its darker occasions. On many days out, I would face some form of abuse, often derision, which whilst sometimes intended to be fun and not malicious, was to me deeply hurtful and at times shook my confidence. Always though, I was to feel the strength of our Father, often through his community in Chiswick and the church where I felt so accepted and supported. If I could be supported by God and those who worshipped Him then I had nothing to fear. The hand of love which Lord Jesus held me with was just so infinitely stronger than the words of hate that mere mortals tried to hit me with.

On one occasion I needed to truly call upon the love and strength of my Lord Jesus. I was in Brighton. I had travelled down to meet a friend and we had dinner at my hotel. She had to leave early so I walked into the bar to have a drink before going to bed. Sitting on my own, I was approached by a couple who invited me to join their friends. 'How nice,' I thought. I sat down and started chatting amiably when one of the friends exploded with a transphobic tirade towards me. I had no escape. I had to listen to this man as he humiliated me, sneered at me, jeered at me, with the whole bar watching. I had been deliberately set up by this 'ever so nice' couple.

I walked away, holding back the anger and tears, trying not to look at anyone for fear of showing my embarrassment, feeling humiliated and belittled. In the privacy of my room, I let the anger boil over and in tears pleaded to my Father for strength. An image swam into my head. It was our Lord Jesus, suffering the humiliation, the jeers, the pain and the execution, for us, for me. Strength flowed back into me. I prayed to our Lord to forgive them.

Not always were Christians so supportive. On one occasion it was someone whose only interaction with me was to come as a guest in my house, on an occasion when we hosted an event to which he had been invited. This event was strongly linked to the church and to a celebration of God's love. He later thanked me for my hospitality by sending me a two-page letter where in almost every line he told me what an abomination to God I was. Fortunately, it was God, or at least His representative in Turnham Green, who answered him and calmed my doubts. Sharing this letter with the priest he read it, shaking his head once or twice. He then folded it back into its envelope, handed it back to me and said, 'Poor man, shall we pray for him?' With those simple words, I found peace.

Despite some setbacks it had been a relatively smooth passage between Jo and I. Jo lived in one side of the house, I lived in the other, but we shared a life also of togetherness, bonded by Gods love that had first tied us together. We were really emerging from darkness. It was time to think about reassignment surgery before the stress of living that lie re-opened some cracks.

I saw a surgeon and after looking at congested diaries we finally agreed on dates. It now could not come quickly enough. Four weeks before surgery, I woke up one morning with an urgent need to go to the loo. However, when I did, I felt a searing pain on urination. My GP made an urgent appointment for me to see a specialist who, having taken all sorts of samples, made an appointment to see me again the following Monday morning.

The weekend came, no respite from the pain and that Saturday evening, I had to go to a party. I scraped myself out of my misery and with a smile on my face, duly honoured my invite and attended, drinking as little as possible both out of respect to my distressed kidney, and out of respect to my own pain thresholds in not wanting to visit the loo that often.

The following day I awoke with a thundering headache. I paid my usual painful visit to the loo and collapsed back in bed. A voice inside was telling me to get up and go to church. I inwardly groaned at the voice and offered a deal to go to the 11:30 service. The voice said no deal; it's got to be the 9:30 service. Anything for a bit of peace I clawed my way out of bed, put a bit of make-up on, painfully threw some clothes on and just made it to the 9:30 service. I walked in to discover it was the one service a month dedicated to prayers of healing. Taking communion, something came over me and I dissolved into tears. I was helped back to my seat and when the service ended, was invited to the back of the church to take prayers with a minister and two prayer leaders. I told them my agony, both physical and mental. Holding me they prayed. I felt a peace come over me.

The following morning, I woke up with two thoughts. The first was go to the loo and collect a sample and the second was getting dressed, as my hospital appointment was for 9 am. Strangely, when I duly collected my sample there was no pain, urination was painless. My headache had also gone.

The specialist was grave of voice. He had the results of tests taken by the doctor a few days earlier. 'I'm sorry, Jennifer, these results clearly show an infection that must be treated as a matter of urgency, and your surgery will have to be cancelled.' I died. If I had no need for surgery, my world would have ended. There was no possible way I could survive any longer with the body I had. I was a monstrously deformed freak who would always be a freak and should be put out of her misery. I could not even cry. My tears had dried up. Crying is for the living, not for the dead, and I might just as well be dead.

I explained my freedom from pain that morning, how the headache had gone, how I felt right again. He smiled sympathetically, gently took the samples from my rigid hand, took them out to the nurse, and then proceeded with a physical examination. Afterwards, he went outside. There was a muffled conversation. He came back in and said he wanted to take more tests. An ultrasound was hastily arranged. He then suggested I make another appointment for the following day when all the results would be available. I shook my head. If I had to sit in the waiting room all night, I would not leave until those results were back.

I waited outside his office. A nurse went in with some papers and then came out again. A dozen patients were seen as I waited. Morning turned to afternoon and afternoon to evening. More patients were seen, more nurses going in and out, and someone I recognised from the first-floor imaging department where I had the ultrasound scan went in, then came out. Then the doctor came out, 'Jennifer, we have all your results.' I went in. He wanted to double-check a few things and do another physical examination. He looked at the ultrasound images and at the laboratory results. He asked me to stick my tongue out again before shaking his head in disbelief. 'Jennifer, I hope you believe in something. All the results are clear, you have had a miracle cure from somewhere.' I smiled. I needed no explanation. I just raised my eyes and whispered to God, 'Thank you for my Lord Jesus.'

Finally, the time came. A friend drove me to Brighton the day before admittance. That night I was to have dinner with Steven my son, but on my way to the hotel, we stopped off at the hospital so my friend could see where to take me the following day. He pulled into the car park and had to keep the car doors locked to prevent me from jumping out and diving into the place and refusing to leave.

Dinner that night was beautiful. My son put his arm around me and said the most magical words, 'To everyone else you are Jenni, and I am proud of you. To me you are Dad, and you will always be my Dad whatever happens.' I blinked the tears back. Steven is not one for great words, but those words meant everything. He may not worship God, but the Holy Spirit was with him that night.

The following morning, I checked in. There was no apprehension, no fear, just excitement that it may soon be over, and peace, along with the knowing that at long last my body and mind would be in harmony. Apart from a few bits and pieces, such as blood samples being taken, there was not much to do, as my surgery was not until the following evening. That afternoon, I asked for a priest to visit me, and we had a service of prayers for healing in the privacy of my room. Again, there was that feeling of knowing I was being looked after, that God was by my side.

I slept well that night. The following morning, I ate all I could before the sign, 'Nil by mouth' was posted on my door. I wished for Jo to be with me, in fact cried inside for her presence, but I knew Jo had to be in Somerset the day before. She was stopping in our flat in London that day and would be visiting the following morning when I was recovering from surgery.

Late morning, a stranger walked into my room. He was another psychiatrist, specialising in gender dysphoria. He was there to satisfy the law. Whilst GD is a medical condition, it is only psychiatrists who can diagnose it, or better, confirm it is not a psychiatric illness, fetish or psychosis presenting itself. By law, anyone about to undergo irreversible changes must obtain a second opinion from someone equally specialised, but totally removed from the patient or the original diagnosing specialist.

During a two-hour interview, he repeatedly told me that I had no need to go through surgery: no one would be upset if I just said I'd changed my mind and was I sure? I sat there in my surgical gown and assured him that I was totally sure. He then asked about aftercare. It will be a stressful time for both me and those caring for me, do we have anyone in our lives strong and supportive. I nodded an affirmative. He needed to emphasise the point, he appeared irritated, and he gave the impression that I was not taking the consequences seriously enough. 'They must be very strong,' he said firmly. I smiled, 'Will God's strength be enough?' I quietly asked.

That afternoon two friends arrived. They had brought Jo with them. It was one of the most beautiful moments of my life to see her walk into that room. The night before, my friends, knowing how desperately I was missing her, had resolved to collect her from the bus station in London when she arrived from Somerset and bring her with them to Brighton.

At 5 pm I got ready, put on the tight embolism prevention socks and for the very last time said goodbye to friends and family in the body I had known for all my life. As I was wheeled into the operating theatre there was only peace and contentment in my heart. My nightmare was about to end.

Chapter 6
A Broken Jigsaw No More

I was struggling to awaken from a deep sleep. The room was strange, cold, coloured in sterile blue shades, with a couple of people in blue loose overalls with what looked to be shower caps on their heads. A strange sight, then my bed was moving, I felt a pain, an uncomfortable burning sensation of wanting to go for a pee. I tried to call out to one of the strange figures in blue, but my voice was so weak and dry that only a feeble croak came out.

A hand gently on my arm, a soft voice. 'It's OK Jenni, that's the catheter, they give that sensation.' The word 'catheter', my bed moving, people in blue overalls with matching shower caps, a sterile room; it all started to fall into place.

Down a corridor, almost awake, into a room I recognised, a room I had been shown into the morning before. The clock said 9:50 pm. Jo and Steven came into the room, Jo with tears of joy and relief in her eyes, holding my arm, kissing me. A nurse on the other side, jabbed a quick, painless injection in my leg and soon the painful burning sensation faded away.

At that moment, I knew. I had been in surgery. At last, I was complete. There was no huge wave of euphoria, no great flood of tears. Instead, there was just a deep internal feeling of comfort, of peace, a peace that Jenni Brown would never again look in the mirror and see a freak. At last, I was a jigsaw of pieces that fitted. For the very first time in the whole of my life, I knew what it was to feel a whole person, not a fragmented collection of parts that never quite fitted together.

Jenni Brown was finally born. It was the most magical feeling of my whole life, simply overwhelming and beautiful. Finally, I was me.

Chapter 7
Return to Normality

Can anyone in their right mind ever admit to being in hospital, recovering from major and radical surgery, having more tubes sticking out of them than they have fingers, being forced to lie flat on their back, restricted to a fluid-only diet and enjoying the experience? I can.

It was not just the excellent nursing care, the surroundings, the quality and care of the surgeon. I was experiencing my own rebirth. I felt as though for the first time in my life, a piece of string could run from the top of my head to the base of my feet and be straight. I was whole, complete, and all connected with every part fitting. I was no longer a jumble of broken and disconnected pieces. For the very first time in the whole of my life, I knew what it was to say, 'I am me.' I no longer felt as though I was something else, or something not quite right, or something that didn't fit.

There were no complications following surgery, not even the most common of post-operative bleeding or minor infections. There was little surgical pain, indeed, my main need for painkillers was caused by backache from having to lie flat, and headache from effectively being on a detox diet. A paracetamol drip coupled with the occasional morphine sufficed to keep the pain away. My first action on being able to leave bed and go for a walk around was to walk to the chapel. I needed to thank someone other than the surgeon and his nurses for my remarkable recovery.

Day seven came and it was time to go home, be with Jo again, and start recovery properly. I was sad to leave. My care, the way I had been looked after, had been magnificent. The pre-admittance guidance notes suggested bringing into the hospital a loose pair of tracksuit bottoms and flat shoes to go home in. I left as I came in; high-heeled boots, a swishy skirt, bright top, hair brushed and make-up on. I felt a million dollars, so I was going to do my best to look it. Amazingly, I had no problems walking normally, a bit slow, and not a lot of energy, but I walked out the same as I walked in.

Steven took me home to my Jo. Our prayers to Jesus, who had held my hand so strongly, were heartfelt and emotional. That evening at 8:30 pm, I was able to go out to dinner with the two amazing friends who had been with me throughout surgery and had taken me to hospital, and then collected Jo and took her to the hospital as well. Less than a week after coming out of the operating theatre, I sat in a restaurant with Jo and two lovely friends having a glass of wine and dinner.

One place I really wanted to go to as soon as strength allowed was over the road from my flat. Walking into Christ Church was so emotional. This had been the church family that had welcomed me when I first walked in with such shyness and trepidation, held me through pain, supported me through torment, reassured me when told what an abomination to God I was and now welcomed me back home as a complete person. As I took my seat the tears would not stop flowing, but they now knew to recognise tears of joy.

My recovery from surgery was rapid, and I thank my Father God for that. If that man who wrote such a cruel letter was right and I am an abomination to God, then God has shown his power to forgive and love even an abomination like me. I believe that I am not an abomination. I am someone born on this earth with a strange and bizarre discrepancy in my makeup and that had been put right. I feel the strength of Jesus and constantly remember the miracle of the unclean woman. So often I find myself muttering the words of Mark 5:34, 'Daughter, your faith has healed you. Go in peace and be freed from your suffering.' It is for Jesus to judge me, and it was my faith in God, for my love for Jesus, to see me through the dark times.

Just four weeks after surgery I returned to duty as a Samaritan volunteer despite being on leave of absence for 13 weeks. It meant so much to be there, giving something back for all I had been given. My return to duty was to only last a few weeks before a burst of hormonal petulance caused us to part company, but I would find other ways to celebrate all that God had given me.

A year after surgery Jo wanted to move home. It was just down the road, somewhere a little more remote, but somewhere not as big and somewhere she felt would give her a fresh start from all the emotional hammer blows she had to deal with. I was still rebuilding my life and a large part of that was in London.

I was having to come to terms with some changes in my life. I do not mean physical ones. There were psychological ones impacting me. One change was my footsteps were lighter, sometimes I would feel as though I was floating, lifted by the sheer peace and joy that I felt inside. Another change was one of confidence. I no longer felt out of step with anyone, I would cheerfully walk in anywhere as a stranger without any nervousness. Another was my faith. It had carried me through everything, I now knew that not only God loves me, both of me, but whatever I did from now on was as His ambassador. As someone that is part of a community so misunderstood, so often reviled, often the butt of sometimes quite cruel humour, how I caried myself in society from now on had to justify that love and grace that I had been so freely given. God loves us all equally and that includes me. God was not only in my life, He was my life.

I was sixty years old when a friend invited me to a dinner. This friend was a historian, had quite an academic background from Cambridge, and we often argued over pivotal moments in history. The dinner was a small one and was being held in a private club in London. The most vocal guest was a doctor somebody who was an historian from an institution somewhere. He spent so much time talking I did not hear the introduction properly and I was barely given an opportunity to clarify. His main interest seemed to be interrogating me, not enjoying his smoked salmon parfait, which I thought was mediocre anyway. No matter how much he wanted to talk he had to wait until I had given grace to God. Some things do come first.

Apparently, he had been impressed by my friend regarding my studies in Virginia. We talked about the First World War, Bismarck's Germany, Krups and the crucial effects the armament manufacturer had on the Franco-Prussian war. By the time we had got onto the beef Wellington I was wishing that the great general himself would burst into the room and stop the interrogation. We had now shifted to 1915 and if there is one person that I would defend historically, it was General Sir Douglas Haig. I argued ferociously he should not be judged for the disasters that befell the British army in that year but instead, his actions seen against the background of the munition shortages, faulty munitions, and wrong types of munitions, all stemming from decisions made in the preceding decades. My argumentative academic friend seemed to be impressed. For my part, I was really pleased for the sorbet to arrive in time to cool us all down.

I was intrigued by this man. Finally, I was to realise that he was a renowned academic and the head of a leading institute specializing in military history. I could forgive him for his persistent interrogation of my views and probing of my knowledge, but I did welcome the generous pouring of the wine, although, like the rest of the dinner, I found it disappointing. I felt like leaving my card in case they wanted a part-time sommelier.

A couple of weeks later I received a call from my friend. Would I like to pop over and see this man, and meet some of his associates at a leading military institute? Ever inquisitive, I said yes, besides, walking into a prestigious military institution with people saluting all over the place would be quite affirming for a newly born trans-woman.

The over-dinner interrogation all became clear when I met them. I was at a job interview. They had a little research project in mind, further investigation into British arms procurement in the intervening years between the rise of the German empire and the outbreak of hostilities in World War 1.

Something strange happened to me. David would have jumped over the table with joy at being given more projects to keep him busy. I had no need of that, the stress of keeping feelings suppressed by constantly being busy was no longer there. In fact, it was quite the opposite. I now wanted time to just enjoy my life, now, so free of stress and so full of joy.

Neither did I need the academic recognition, the University of Virginia had given me that. By sheer coincidence, they had given me, via that, a place to study in a military academy, for it was at the Virginia Military Institute that I had done most of my writing and research. What I wanted most in those days, so soon after surgery, was affirmation of me as a trans-woman. The promised place at the Institute for Historical Research in London would give me that.

I agreed but on my terms. It would be freelance, not tied to any institute or university, and quite free to walk away should our opinions differ on certain strongly held views. I also wanted time to pursue possible charitable projects with Christian organisations, I had a lot to give thanks for. This they found acceptable. I distinctly got the feeling that the last thing they wanted was the university supervising the project and actively interfering in it. They were, therefore, quite enthusiastic about my strong stance. However, a senior academic representative from that university was there, and she immediately launched a hostile interrogation towards me, indicating that she really felt they needed more control than I was prepared to agree to.

A few times I was tempted to get up and walk out, but weathered the storm until lunch was called. During much of the onslaught I just closed my eyes and prayed, for guidance, for strength and for other things, but the head of department for making lightning bolts must have been on holiday and so none rained down on her head.

I walked into the dining hall determined to sit as far away from this woman as possible. Glaring daggers at her I moved to one end of the table, but she made sure that we sat together. Towards the end of lunch, she grabbed my arm, 'Sorry about that,' she said and then went on to explain. 'You are going to need to be on the top of your game, you are walking into a possible hornet's nest of misogyny, you must be prepared to stand your ground, be firm, fight your corner. It can be a hostile place for women such as you and me.' I pinched myself, did I really hear that right? 'For women such as you and me'? I had yearned for affirmation and the academic battle-axe had just given it to me.

It never really got off the ground. There were arguments between sponsors, academic institutions and military academies, combined with a certain lack of interest from myself. Whilst others argued over format and content, I wandered around the institute finding lots of other things to entertain me, some great lectures and lecturers, and even found myself included on the speaker panel talking about migrations of peoples across the USA and campaigns of the American Civil War.

Life was settling down. Jo was very busy with our new home in Somerset, and very busy with her church. She had been appointed as church warden and as the regular congregation was only a small one, she had a lot of other jobs to do as well. Before we moved house, we hosted Alpha courses in our home and whilst now we were too far from the church to do that, it was still an involvement for Jo. People would remark on her strength but we both knew where it came from. The love of Jesus had been poured over us both.

I was also finding that the stares, sneers and abusive comments were becoming infrequent. It was never very great but sometimes just one bit of abuse in what has been a bad week could be quite distressing. Now it was rare. It was time to move to the last step, the gender recognition certificate, or GRC, for short.

The GRC is an essential safeguard. Without it, despite all my other documents recording me as female, the state would always consider me as male. The GRC changes all my state documents from social security to the birth certificate and gives me a lot of legal protection against disclosure of my medical history, and my previous identity, intentional or otherwise. However, there was to be a most painful cost. The state, by recognising me as female, would demand annulment of my marriage, as once a GRC had been issued, we would be in a same-sex marriage, something prohibited by law.

The original draft of the Gender Recognition Act followed procedures adopted by other countries, in providing an exemption for couples who had been married for over a certain length of time. This exemption had been opposed by several denominations of churches. The UK at the time was one of only three European countries, and one of only a handful in the world, which did not have gender recognition legislation and felt under pressure to catch up, so it dropped the exemption. Jo and I had to go through the terrible pain, and considerable expense, of annulling nearly forty years of marriage. It was not a divorce, it had to be an annulment, a declaration that the marriage was illegal in the first place.

It had been our vows, and our love between us, that had been the glue that had kept us together during the most destructive of times. We made those vows in front of God; they were sacrosanct to us. Man might be the one to want to put asunder, but Jo and I preferred the Matthew 19:6 version of, 'Let no man put asunder.' If we cannot retain our original marriage certificate, we could continue to legalise our relationship through a civil partnership. In fact, financially it was a necessity for as soon as the annulment was made absolute, we would be treated as just friends by HMRC and any transfer of assets between us considered to be a gift for inheritance or Capital Gains Tax.

For Jo this was awful. She reluctantly accepted the compromise but felt she had to confide to her church vicar how painful, petty and spiteful she felt it all to be. The Civil Partnership Act was established to enable same-sex couples to solemnise their relationship and share the same legal protections that married couples had, but she was a heterosexual woman being forced into a partnership that was a platonic one. The priest was sympathetic and comforted Jo by saying we will always be sisters in Christ. It was how Jo wanted others to see our relationship, as sisters, not as a same-sex couple. Even this was to cause ripples with the church further down the road.

The whole process was supposed to be seamless, the same judge whilst declaring the annulment absolute, also issues the GRC, so a civil partnership can be enacted immediately. No one told our local registrar. In fact, no one told me that the marriage had been annulled. My first clue was when the Department of Work and Pensions dropped me a line telling me that my pension was to be paid from the age of sixty, not sixty-five.

We contacted the local registrar who needed time to both get a copy of my GRC and to get hold of some guidance notes. We were also no longer legally a couple, so Jo searched the internet for rolls of protective bubble wrap to encase me in, until we were legally joined back again.

It was a Wednesday. We had a variety of people in our house. My secretary, Jo's gardener and a stonemason friend who was building a terrace for us. Collected in the kitchen for a cup of coffee I was regaling them with the sad story of annulment. The gardener, holding a pot of wilting flowers, shook his head and said he didn't know what to say. Jo wanted to say something about the shower of compost falling onto her carpet. Our stonemason friend just looked on in despair, as a piece of mortar dripped off his trowel onto the floor. My secretary busied herself making a cup of tea. Jo continued popping bubble wrap.

The phone rang. It was the registrar. She had read the guidance notes, if I could cobble a wedding party together, we could be rejoined now. The mood in the kitchen lifted. We all grabbed a wilting flower from the gardeners' pot and stuffed it into whatever buttonhole we could find. We needed two best people and a witness. The gardener put down his pot and climbed into my car as the best person, my secretary put down the kettle and climbed into my car as a witness, and the stonemason, still with the trowel in his hand, climbed into my car as the other best person. I started to set off but realised someone was missing. As an afterthought, I grabbed Jo, put down the bubble wrap, and the wedding party set off. An hour later we were civil partners. A painful chapter had reached its conclusion.

We both craved time to settle. It had been ten years of emotional turmoil, the quite awful passage of time when I was in meltdown and Jo being so cruelly treated, of the revelation of gender dysphoria and where it could lead, the tentative steps to see if we could make the transition work between us, the transition itself and now the legal conclusions coming to their seemingly spiteful end. It was an end when we were both stronger, where we had felt the full glow of God's love and where our church and church families had been so strong for us.

However, a small spot inside my nose was going to continue to give us pain and uncertainty for a few more years. I had become aware of it when hay fever seemed remorseless, and I had asked a doctor for advice. He spotted it and sent me to an ENT man, the same man I had met before during abortive attempts to make my voice an octave or two higher. 'Harmless little wart,' he said.

Two weeks later, after having had the harmless little wart removed under general anaesthetic, my phone rang. It was the surgeon giving me the glad tidings that the dear harmless thing was in fact cancerous. I needed to get back to him as soon as possible for explorative surgery.

The explorative surgery revealed more bits of cancerous growth, and it was back in again for more lumps to be chopped off inside my nose and sinuses. He could never understand why I was so calm about it. I just knew that God would either guide the surgeon's hand successfully or I would be joining God in his kingdom. Either way, it was a no-lose situation.

It was to get worse. My nose was looking mangled. I decided to go for cosmetic surgery to repair my nose and soften some of my facial features. It was a long job, eleven hours, the best specialist in Europe by reputation, was in Belgium and it was the coldest winter ever. Jo came with me, and it all went well. The following day I was allowed to leave hospital and return to our hotel. We both gave thanks to God that night. Neither of us realised how much prayer we would need the following day.

I woke up in the middle of the night with an itch. By 5 am it was driving me nuts, so much so that I had sat in a bath for half an hour. By six in the morning, large lumps of skin were blistering and peeling. By seven I was barely coherent and barely conscious. Jo called a taxi to get me to the hospital, but he took us to the wrong hospital. Despite her limitations in speaking Flemish or Dutch, she had managed to get the wrong hospital to give directions to the right hospital. By now I was wandering in and out of unconsciousness and my breathing was becoming laboured.

At the right hospital, I was taken into an emergency room. Various doctors were called including an anaesthetist, should I need to have a breathing tube inserted. Eventually, I was stabilised, anaphylactic shock diagnosed and taken off all painkillers and antibiotics until the cause was found.

Three days later, a lot of calling on God's grace and I was released from hospital. Getting home was difficult but again a stroke of luck, or God's help, a seat was found on an airplane travelling from Antwerp to London City airport. It was fortuitous, for a rail accident at Brussels a few days earlier had left Eurostar cancelled and flights between Belgium and the UK were seriously in demand. Apparently, a cancellation just a few minutes earlier had created just one empty seat on the airplane. The airline sales agent's joy at so quickly selling a cancelled place was then dashed when advised it was a medical evacuation and now, they need to find room for my carer, even if it meant bumping someone else off the plane!

We arrived home in Chiswick and once Jo was sure that I was recovering, she set off for home. I stared out of the window at her going and just felt so lonely. I went to church that Sunday and prayed to Jesus, to hold my hand and give me direction. I came back home, looked around and decided I no longer needed a place in London. My place was with Jo.

Jo was not so enthusiastic. We had spent most of our married years with me spending some time away, either for a few days or sometimes for a few weeks. She knew also that I did not enjoy the rural secluded life as much as she did, I was highly gregarious and needed people around me. Perhaps wait a while before giving up our London home.

It was a fortuitous wait. A few months later I felt a lump inside my nose. With trepidation, I returned to the ENT surgeon and went to sleep on Valentine's Day 2012, whilst he removed the offending lump. The histology proved the worst, the cancer had returned, had changed tissue type and was in a far more dangerous position. It had to go and radiotherapy was the follow-up.

I was having radiotherapy at a hospital near to the Institute for Historic Research. Being ever efficient, I planned one session for a day when I would be giving a lecture there. I had my session, then had a cup of coffee and a couple of glasses of water at a nearby café. Feeling a bit bedraggled, I made my way to the institute, read my notes, checked my PowerPoint list, then went into the room where I would be speaking. I put my notes on the lectern and started talking. As I did so the lights at the back of the room started to brighten and then spin round. 'Strange,' I thought as the lectern toppled off the stage, me following it, but fortuitously held from falling, by the two people who had just finished introducing me.

An hour later I sat in a taxi going home after being cleared to leave the building by two paramedics. I returned to my flat. I sat there in my empty box, alone, no Jo. My mind went back to that awful time when I last sat in a flat alone, in secret. My dreadful lie was being concealed from the person that I loved the most, the person who above all others, had been so strong when the awful truth came tumbling out. I had to start disentangling my life in London, which was the past. The future was with Jo and I living a completely new life together. There was only one person I could get help from. My mind pleaded with our Father, to show me the way. I needed not to have worried. Jesus still had a firm grip on my hand.

The following day I contacted an estate agent to start the process of selling my London property. She was not the agent that rented my flats in the property, the natural choice to approach, but for some strange reason I went to this other agency. I knew enough now to know that when strange reasoning happens, to just let it happen, for this could be God's way, this could be Jesus leading me.

She knew of someone who would be interested but now was not the time. It would be a few months before that person would have their own affairs in order before they could consider another purchase. As always, that confirmed that Jesus was holding my hand for it could not happen immediately from my end. I had to let Jo warm to the idea of living with me full time first, no easy task, and I had a lot of loose ends to tidy up. My approach to this estate agent, who had a probable buyer in the wings, was perfect timing.

That Autumn I received brilliant news. My third visit to the ENT surgeon after surgery and radiotherapy, and smiles all around, no signs of anything returning. Time to think again about getting out of London. I now only had our house and was using one of the flats to stop over when in London. The place was looking tatty, the whole building needed a makeover to freshen it up, but I just couldn't be bothered. The last few years of almost constant surgery had left me desperately weak physically and mentally. I quit the institute. I also quit a voluntary role that I had held for seven years with the Imperial War Museum. I quit many of the social functions that I was associated with. There was just one other formal activity that I was involved in that took me to London, but I did not need a residence to fulfil only that one. I could manage quite happily with a hotel room.

I called the estate agent and was told that the buyer she had spoken of a few months earlier was now ready to view and keen to agree on a deal. I prepared to live full-time in the rural emptiness that Jo called home. In my head I knew that it would be difficult, I needed to see people every day and wanted other facilities near me than just a village shop, a pub and a mobile chippy that called whenever he felt like stopping, which was not that often. My heart though could no longer take the loneliness of being apart from Jo on a regular basis after we had both fought almost impossible odds to stay together. I had to trust in my faith in Jesus, that He will be our guide. I did not have long to wait for further proof that the hand of Jesus was leading me.

Jo and I have a lot of family in the Shoreham area of the South Coast. Our son Steven with his partner lives there, so does my sister Barbara. We have nieces, nephews and grandnieces and nephews there, and I was in London a couple of weeks before Christmas when I popped down to visit my sister. Having had a big family gathering on the Friday, I was due to have a quiet dinner with my son and his partner on the Saturday. After dinner, we sat in the bar having a drink and he said, 'We have a photo to show you.' It was an ultrasound picture. 'Don't tell anyone yet,' he shouted to me as I dashed to the loo. Too late. Jo's phone was already ringing as I prepared to give her the news that she was going to be a grandma.

Jo and I were ecstatic. We just seemed to keep wandering around the house praising our Father God at every opportunity. It was totally unexpected, we had both resigned ourselves to the fact they were happy as a childless couple. It even took my mind away for a while thinking about the thorny issue of me getting out of London, and moving to the home that I shared with Jo full-time. Again, that reminder that Jesus, our Saviour, was leading us to peace, a final peace and contentment together.

Part two of God answering my prayers came a few weeks later. We went for Christmas to visit family on the South Coast. It is a part of the country that Jo did not like. Too many people, too overcrowded, too much housing, too flat were the main reasons expressed by the rural-emptiness, solitude-loving, welly-wearing Jo. We stopped in a hotel outside Shoreham and invited the family to come and have dinner with us. Of course, it was Steven and his partner that Jo wanted to see most and keeping silent about the amazing news was something she found difficult.

Coming home was difficult. Our main roads home was on the A27, M27 and A303 but huge congestion on the A27 from Worthing, all the way to Arundel, made me look for an alternative route. I chose a nice meandering route through the small towns and villages along the crest of the South Downs National Park, to rejoin the A27 west of the town of Arundel. It was a most pleasant afternoon and the South Downs sparkled in the weak winter sunshine.

Jo was part mumbling to herself and part mumbling to me. 'This is nice,' 'I think I could live here,' 'Probably very expensive,' 'But I could definitely think of moving here', and finally, 'What do you think Jen'? Jen was thinking all sorts of things, in fact, Jen's head was exploding with possibilities. 'Very nice Jo, but you love where you are, let's just get home.'

We arrived home. Jo thought I was being uncharacteristically rude, for the first thing I did was open my laptop. She unpacked and then tried to get my attention. 'Jen, what do you think, what I mentioned this afternoon?' I grunted, then got back to my laptop. 'Jen, I'm serious, Jen, it's important we talk, seriously, I think that I could move, that I could live there, can we talk about it, JEN! PLEASE, PUT YOUR LAPTOP AWAY AND LISTEN!' 'Sorry Jo,' I said, showing her the screen. I was on websites called Zoopla and Rightmove, doing a little spot of house-hunting!

Part three was finding the place right for us both. The peace and contentment we both craved, and which we knew Jesus was leading us to, would only be achieved by finding what in time would satisfy the needs of us both. Jo had said that she would look at houses, not promising anything, but only within ten miles of the address of a growing family. I went back to Rightmove, drew my circle, and off I went, stage one of my new research project.

There was not a lot to look at. I assumed Jo wanted a rural location but most of the rural locations were outside of the 10 mile radius. There were a couple of villages, but I had had enough of one-horse towns, or small one pub, one-chippy villages. I came back with details of three, one on the west side of Worthing, and if you stood on tiptoe and looked out of a top-floor dormer window you could just about glimpse open countryside. Another was a bit less rural but did back onto a golf course, and one was very suburban but did have fake half-timbers so did look a bit rural. There was another house whose details cropped up every time I searched, but it was thirteen miles away, to me it looked 'wonky' and was in a village location, too far for Jo and the last thing I wanted was a village.

I returned from my voyage of discovery only to see Jo deposit the details of three houses in the bin. What she said next floored me and made sure my next trip planning had to start from scratch again. 'If I'm going to live on the South Coast then I want to live on the coast, not five miles from it, standing on tiptoe to see a glimpse of a tree.'

Crestfallen, I returned to my digital search engine. I put the cursor on Shoreham Beach and drew a ten-mile radius. Eastwards took me to Brighton and beyond. Somewhere definitely not for me, for during transition I had experienced some very difficult times in Brighton. Westwards took me to Worthing. Even though I had dictated to the search engine, 'ten miles maximum' it took me well beyond Worthing. The only problem was that my car did not fly like a crow and what took the crow ten miles to fly, would take me fifteen miles to drive due to the vagaries of the road network. Despite that there were some very attractive houses west of Worthing, but again the wonky house turned up and I didn't want to live in a village with just wonky houses and no restaurants, pubs or people, so I ignored it.

Nonetheless, I set off on another voyage of discovery, this one skirting the channel coast. I returned triumphant. My arms were full of details of lovely houses. Jo must surely be impressed.

My elation turned to despair as she thumbed through them. 'Not enough bedrooms,' 'Can't live with that kitchen,' 'Oh goodness, how can they call three embedded paving slabs a patio,' and 'Won't even get a microwave in that utility.' I sat in despair as the bin filled up.

Next attempt and it was the digital world getting binned. I sent a snail mail to two estate agents on the coast. It was precise, detailing numbers of bedrooms, sizes of reception rooms and even how many cars could we get on the drive. As I affixed the stamps, I sent a prayer upwards that I may find the right house.

A few days later two envelopes clattered to the floor via our letterbox. With trepidation, I opened them. Jo put the kettle on and together, over a cup of tea, and with mounting excitement, we read the details. Each had details of two houses. The first two out of the envelopes were different from each other but no different to what I had viewed for what seemed a thousand times over. The next two were the same. It was the wonky house. Clearly, someone was trying to tell me something and it was not for me to question; my faith was with my Saviour and guide! I made an appointment to view a house that I would never have considered, had it not been for the multiple nudges prompting us to keep on the right track.

The night before viewing I drove down to Shoreham, booked into a nice hotel a few miles North of town and had a most pleasant dinner with many members of my extended family. The next morning, I woke early, I do not sleep well in hotels, and despite my appointment not being until mid-morning, I set off at the crack of dawn.

I took a circuitous route towards my destination, I might as well explore the area, and around 9 am found myself in the small village of Angmering. This was not my idea of a village, it had two pubs, not one, a chippy but also a co-op and a church. Sussex villages had a lot more in them than Somerset villages. As a church was of equal importance to the house, I decided to have a look. There were quite a few people standing around but then it was a Sunday. I asked about times of service and was told one was about to start. Well, why not, I still had plenty of time to spare.

It was a lovely service. I really enjoyed it. Everyone was friendly and the service was lively, just what Jo and I enjoy. I shook hands with the vicar who welcomed me as someone new to the church. I had not even had time to ask the name of the church, and the vicar looked a bit surprised when I asked him 'Where am I?,' but he informed me that I was at St Margaret's. I nearly fell over. Jo's favourite church, which she drove some distance to get to every Sunday, was also St Margaret's. Now I knew it was meant to be.

I drove to my appointment. As I entered the 'village' I was pleasantly surprised. There was a row of shops, and I was used to driving five miles just to get to the nearest local minimart. As for supermarkets, I had already ascertained that Sainsbury's had a superstore only a couple of miles away, whereas I was used to driving fourteen miles to get to one. I passed a British Legion branch, always a good source of lively entertainment, a couple of hundred yards further on and another row of shops, including the mandatory chippy, two pubs, a restaurant, a couple of cafes, a hotel further down with a licensed bar and restaurant. This place was beginning to grow on me.

I found somewhere to park and decided to go for a walk. I asked someone how I could get to the beach. Their expression was one of amusement. Ten yards and I was on it, and the greensward, a wide expanse of grass running alongside it. This was doggy heaven and my thoughts turned towards our menagerie of dogs who would be in heaven running freely along here.

I looked at my map and realised the house I was due to view was only 250 yards up from the beach. Now I was really beginning to like this place. I turned up for the appointment, my feet crunching on the shingle drive. I do not like loose surfaces, the small shingle attaches to feet and tyres and soon disappears, often into the carpet inside the house. It was not a good start.

I rang the bell, the door opened, and I was greeted by a vista not uncommon to that of a post-war pawn shop. The two people who owned the house had formed a partnership late in life, when both had accrued a substantial quantity of artefacts and now these artefacts filled every room, practically floor to ceiling. Talking of ceiling, chandeliers hung down from every light point, by the time I had walked the length of the hallway, bruises were starting to appear all over my forehead.

I was shown into what they called the music room, an apt description for it housed enough musical instruments to supply a symphony orchestra. I was told that French doors led to the garden and by stepping around a double bass, avoiding putting my foot into the mouth of a tuba and climbing over a piano, I could see that was right. I was shown into the dining room, important to us for one of our prized possessions was a beautiful 11ft long dining table, but whilst the floor plan suggested it would fit comfortably, I could not see the floor and did not get that impression.

Despite the clutter, the house slowly started to make sense. Reading the details would give the impression of a house designed by someone deranged, who builds a house with three staircases in it for example? Slowly it dawned on me, that this house, one that I had rejected repeatedly from just reading the details, a house I was only viewing because someone kept insisting that I did, was in fact perfect for us.

It had evolved over three distinct periods of development, hence the three staircases. Staircase one led to a distinct two-bedroomed area, one en-suite, and a bathroom at the end of a short hallway. Perfect for me, a bedroom with a study opposite that could serve as a guest bedroom with its own bathroom on the same floor. A second development had been added with an additional sitting room, and above this was an en-suite bedroom plus a small nursery bedroom, somewhere a yet unborn child could sleep, next to an adoring Grandma. Jo's side came into view.

The third part of the house was an annexe tacked onto the side, a garage downstairs, kitchen behind and the third staircase, leading to two bedrooms and a bathroom. I thought of a family in Shoreham with a child on the way. Perfect.

The final cherry on the cake was a junk room just off the downstairs hallway. This had a sink in it and was directly opposite a downstairs cloakroom. One of the owners explained that his dad often stayed in there. He was quite frail and could not manage steps but the basin inside and the toilet opposite meant he could use it as a short-term bedroom. I saw the basin, envisaged an en-suite bathroom and thought of our frail Mum, virtually immobilised from strokes, and my brother-in-law with a deteriorating spinal condition.

I left to go home in a bit of a daze. This was a house that I would never have considered viewing had it not been for the details repeatedly coming up on every search, and for estate agents sending those details despite it being outside my stated area of search. I thought of that prayer as I posted the snail mail to those estate agents, I thought of the often heard phrase, 'Give your problems to the Lord', I thought of the church called St Margaret's. I drove home almost shaking my head in disbelief at the power of our Father God.

I returned home trying to conceal my excitement. I wanted Jo to view and not be influenced by me. 'It's probably ok,' I said, 'You do need to see for yourself.' Jo came. She seemed to do a strange dance around the house, first hopping over one artefact before bobbing down under a bone-shattering chandelier.

Finally, we left, in silence, both of us with our own thoughts. Turning a corner away from the house I pulled over to the side of the road. 'What do you think?' I said. I thought she looked a bit dazed but had put that down to the collection of bruises now appearing on her forehead. 'I could live there,' she said. That was all I needed to hear. I drove to the estate agent. Parked up outside we had another conversation. Yes, we were both sure. We walked in, made an offer and bought the house.

Moving into that house, moving away from where so much pain and heartbreak had happened, gave us a new beginning. For almost the first time since we were married, there were no distractions to take me away for a few days. Jo stressed that she needed that time on her own, a break from the high-octane Jen. I agreed, bought a camper, and for the next few years popped away for a few days every month to explore both the British Isles and Europe, in fact, I got to just love the Channel tunnel.

Jo's mum, the person I had so grown to love and also called mum, grew weaker. Now, I was not going away on my own so much, and if I went I had Jo with me, staying in the nearest B&B accommodation that I could find close to where I parked up. Then another brainwave, get a caravan, that way we could be together on the same campsite. Now, I was going away, not on my own, not just with Jo beside me, but now every time I looked in the rearview mirror, I could see her bedroom bobbing along behind mine!

This is just a measure of how much our love has grown, that we now want to be together so much. The love that was so tested during many dark years, that kept us together as we forged a new relationship that carried us through so many stressful times afterwards, is now as strong as it ever was or could ever be, and for that we thank our Lord Jesus.

Chapter 8
For the Love of Jesus

How time can move us on. It is now over ten years since we moved into the house that Jesus led us to, where He knew we would be happy. It is 20 years since that evening, walking home in the pouring rain, shaken to my very core about how close I came to destroying myself, that the strength and love of our Lord Jesus pulled me away from destruction. Walking home in that pouring rain passing those words, adorning a poster hanging from the railings of Christ Church Turnham Green. The poster words from Acts, 'Believe in the Lord Jesus and you will be saved,' how that hit home and how I was to repeat them so often in the next twenty years.

Of course, this story does not begin 20 years ago, nor does it begin 21 years ago when I opened a door and found the light of Jesus still there, illuminating my life. It begins when I was born, or as some experts believe, a few months before I was born. It is in those first years a story of the simplest faith, of how just a very simple faith kept a young child alive, both mentally and physically, and for long enough for that child to reach an age where it could take responsibility for itself.

The child, now as human adult but still a child of God, then let go of the hand that had so supported him. In letting go I opened the door to many years of anguish, pain and misery, punctuated often with moments of human joy, but always spiritually hungry and empty. Without that hand to guide me I sunk deeper and deeper into a morass of confusion, mental and physical exhaustion, alcohol abuse, blindly thrashing around trying to find solutions to a question that I could not even ask truthfully of myself. What was the cause of that inner turmoil and anguish that allowed me no peace? At this point, without Jesus, I was not even me, the person I know now.

Then I allowed the love of Jesus to come back into my life. The darkest of times were about to be encountered, the depths of despair were to be felt, but it was that love and certainty of guidance that carried me through those darkest times.

I prayed to be shown the cause of the anguish that had blighted most of my life and the answer was to lead me down a road that I doubted I would ever have the strength to complete. That I did travel that road to the end was only because of the strength of Jesus leading me, and at times carrying me, but how smoother would that road have been had my faith been stronger?

I doubted the love of others to stay with me, but what I really doubted was my faith. Had I been firmer of faith I would never have doubted for I would have seen that others also shared the love of Jesus, and they too would be led and supported as I had been.

As others poured scorn, as some took it upon themselves to assume God's voice of condemnation, so the love of Jesus supported me, and the suffering inflicted upon my Lord Jesus gave me the strength and will to forgive. However, I am only human and will also say that sometimes words of forgiveness were coloured by thoughts I am now ashamed of, thoughts of spite and vengeance.

Over half a century ago I made vows in front of God, vows to honour, to obey and to let no man put asunder. No man did, although some tried, but no man will ever be stronger than God's love that binds us together. Jo and I are as happy together now as we have ever been, and as long as we can revel in the knowledge of the love of Jesus so we will continue to be.

That church, the one I did not even know the name of when I first stepped inside to worship, has become a rock to us both. We are part of a beautiful church family and have found a place to worship and give thanks for all we know we have been given. Some will call it a coincidence that led me to find it in the first place. I can only smile when I think of the coincidence as I know it was the hand of Jesus that led me there.

As for the wonky house, the house I was led to when God decided he had to intervene in the estate agency business. For a few short years, it gave us somewhere that a frail old Mum could come and stay until a frail old Mum was quite deservedly called to go to be with God and to be bathed in the love of Jesus. It continues to give us somewhere where now two young grandchildren can come for a sleepover, and it regularly rings with the sound of children's laughter.

It is also a house that plays host for a day, the Holy Spirit day after an Alpha course, and a house, where others have found the resolve to say, 'I will give myself to Jesus', words that brought the greatest love and strength into my life over 20 years ago.

I will not dwell on the bigotry and prejudice I have had to face and overcome, and occasionally still face, simply because an adult is ignorant of facts or does not have the will to accept them. Two young children have given me the most beautiful riposte to all that nonsense.

They know Jo as Grandma, something they could not call me for I am not a grandma. However, when I offered to be called, 'Aunty Jen' their lovely mum rejected it, I was a grandparent, not an aunty, so, I became known as Granny Jen.

Two young, inquisitive minds put two and two together and answered a conundrum, why they have two grandmas, and a granny, but only one grandad? A little while ago, I was approached by two curious little children. The eldest one said, 'Granny Jen, can I ask a question?' I smiled, and answered, 'Of course,' after all, who could deny a child a question even if I felt I knew what it would be.

'Were you once a boy?' said a little voice, '…and are you my Daddy's Daddy?' said the other little voice. 'Yes' I said, 'but an illness meant I had to change from boy to girl.' Two smiles creased two little faces that was it, mystery solved. Next problem. 'Can you take us to the beach now, Granny Jen?'

If only adults could retain the unconditional and non-judgmental love of a child.

www.ingramcontent.com/pod-product-compliance
Lightning Source LLC
Chambersburg PA
CBHW041147110526
44590CB00027B/4159